"In a sea of drab and monotonous leadership book[...] one that will not only catapult your leadership skills to the next level but entertain you at the same time."

—Justin Volrath, SVP of Sales at Beyond Payments

"Markwardt's leadership resembles a coach who can push an elite athlete to the peak of their game. He details all of his insights through this guidebook to grow leaders. His concepts told through the Leadership Wheel provide a road map to success for everyone at any level of their career."

—Bill Schuffenhauer, 2002 Olympic Silver Medalist, Motivational Speaker, Small Business Owner

"Markwardt provides concrete strategies on how to create a vision and associated tactics on engaging and enrolling a team, all the while cleverly wrapped in an on-the-road travelogue. This is a must-read for all managers."

—Pat Helmers, Host of the Sales Babble Podcast

"This is not your average business book. Markwardt teaches leadership concepts while taking you on a travel adventure. The end result is not only entertaining but the ultimate playbook to develop leaders to the highest level."

—Ryan Thorne, Senior Sales Leader, Fortune 1000 Company

Grow into an Elite Leader

The Grass Is Browner on the Other Side

▶ LEADERSHIP EDITION ◀

JON MARKWARDT

KNIGHT
BUSINESS PRESS

SAN FRANCISCO

THE GRASS IS BROWNER ON THE OTHER SIDE ® LEADERSHIP EDITION

Neither the publisher nor the author is engaged in rendering legal or other professional services through this book. If expert assistance is required, the services of an appropriate competent professional should be sought. The author and publisher shall have neither liability nor responsibility to any person or entity with respect to any loss or damage caused, or alleged to have been caused, directly or indirectly by the information contained in this book. Some names and details have been changed within the context of the stories to protect the privacy of the individuals being discussed.

Inquiries: www.GrassIsBrowner.com

Paperback: 978-0-9978580-3-7

Kindle: 978-0-9978580-4-4

Cataloging in Publication Data on file with Publisher

Publishing and production: Concierge Marketing Inc.

Illustrated by Penelope Constantinou, Nicosia, Cyprus, www.penelope-art.net

Graphic Design for Leadership Wheel by Kelly Henderson, San Francisco, CA, www.KLNDesign.com

Photographs of Jon Markwardt by Arda Aytan, Istanbul, Turkey, www.ardaaytan.com

Printed in the United States of America

10 9 8 7 6 5 4 3 2 1

To Steven Junor

You've taught me more about attitude in the battle of your glioblastoma than anyone could ever learn from a book, mentor or elite leader. Ultimately, everyone's attitude is a choice. Thank you for having the strength to stay positive and inspire those around you. Your encouragement for me to continue my career as an author led to the adventures in this book. You provide an important leadership lesson prior to Chapter 1. Stay positive, and love your life. Love you, buddy!

Contents

The Quest for Leadership

My first book was written for sales professionals looking to grow their careers. Equally important are the people managing those individuals. This book was written for those looking to take on leadership roles, active managers and respected leaders striving to grow to an elite level. While the concepts in this book are catered to the sales profession, elite leadership principles are applicable across all platforms.

There are many managers in the workforce, but there are not enough leaders who provide learning and growth for each person on their team. The *Grass Is Browner* concept is especially powerful for leaders able to create this environment. This is produced by providing a culture of not wanting to go anywhere else, which equates to the greenest grass on the block. These employees will learn, grow and better their careers exactly where they are at.

Grass Is Browner is a philosophy you are able to embrace for your career and personal life. This philosophy encourages you to believe you are in the best position. There is not greener grass on the other side, because you only have the moment you are in. This mantra encourages you to love the position you are in and grow your green grass. Your yard and life can and will be an example of success for everyone to admire.

Too often managers become overly concerned with day-to-day tasks and forget to concentrate on creating this environment for their team. They stop caring about each person individually and only care about reports, activity levels, and their own quota. When a manager's only concern is themselves, the atmosphere on the team shifts to a *Grass Is Greener* effect as their team searches for new opportunities.

A team determined to water their own grass will provide a leader with one requirement for securing an elite team. Tenure. But how is this practice created? And how does a leader truly effect the culture of a team? These questions will help us focus on the differences between a boss and a leader as we navigate through this book together.

Most often, the first leaders we have in our lives are our parents. From there, we have other family members and friends inserted as we start to expand our leadership network. Eventually, we grow older and the number of leaders and influencers in our lives stretch far beyond the initial bubble of our parents and immediate family.

My own quest for leadership is a personal journey to know the leaders I came from. My great-grandfather immigrated to the United States from an unknown town in East Germany at the beginning of the twentieth century, but the details of our family history are foggy at best. The specifics are incomplete due to language barriers and not knowing where to search. With my grandfather, Ken Markwardt, approaching his ninetieth birthday, I felt an urgency to find and visit the town his father came from. My goal is to bring more of this history to life for him and my family.

In an age of instant knowledge on our phones, tablets and personal computers; it is growing seemingly rare to not be able to find factual answers to our questions. While it is common to not know where your family came from, this answer could not be found on the internet. To find answers to the mystery of where my surname originated, I would need to do far more than a Google search.

Authenticity and unusual analogies are an important part of my writing. And this expedition met these criteria to articulate leadership concepts. Consequently, the search for my family history is the premise of my travels and writing for the entire book.

I believe in order to be successful, we must be in a constant state of learning. While I have spent my entire career in sales and leadership positions, I am continually looking to learn and grow my own knowledge on this subject. This story is not about finding a town, my great-grandfather's birth certificate or tracking down a distant relative. The narrative is a tale of adjusting my life and schedule quickly for the greater good of the book. This allows me to tackle the subject matter like an elite leader who continually shifts focus for the benefit of their team.

I believe a lot can be learned from visiting new places and people. Therefore, I will allow my travels to take me outside of my desired destinations for the purpose of collecting leadership concepts along the way. I plan to interview three recognizable leaders on my travels as they share their top leadership characteristics and describe examples of how these traits have impacted their careers.

Markwardt's Wheel of Leadership is a chart designed to outline the necessary components for an elite sales leader to build and operate their team. I will detail each section of this Wheel throughout our journey. Retaining your employees and completing the entire Wheel is no easy task. Elite leadership requires a commitment to the long-term as the Wheel will never be achieved by an overnight sprint.

We are in a society constantly searching for the next best thing. Careers once operating in a format of hire to retire are no longer the norm. In order to retain your best individuals, it is imperative learning and growth occur. This will be a theme in the book and the center of the Leadership Wheel.

My ultimate mission is to provide you with entertaining stories for established leadership concepts to illustrate the social and business proof for each chapter. You may find yourself reading an unusual story that you believe has nothing to do with growing into an elite leader. When this occurs, please know you will find a point to the story later on. The key is to keep reading as the adventures herein will allow each leadership concept to be better understood and remembered.

Furthermore, I don't like to travel alone. Growing into an elite leader is a journey in itself, so this book will allow us to travel on a leadership quest together. Now as my travel partner, it's time for us to go adventure!

1

Midnight Sun

Markwardt's Wheel of Leadership was created for you to recognize your own needs as a leader, achieve them and coach your people to progress their career in a similar fashion. Whether your needs are being met or you are striving for growth in the company to achieve your needs, this Leadership Wheel will be your greatest measurement of success. Building the entire Wheel will result in growing your career to be among a small group of leaders considered elite.

The outer circle of the Leadership Wheel defines the requirements for elite leadership to occur. And the center places the greatest need of a leader as their ability to create an environment where employees can learn and grow. But learning and growth will not properly occur with a manager in place. Therefore, it is important to establish the six attributes necessary for leadership. Care, trust, attitude, preparation, communication and urgency are the characteristics necessary for an individual to grow into an elite leader.

A leader is constantly moving and shifting focus to take care of the needs for their team. They operate like a wheel in motion to create progress and success. Take a moment to look at the entire Wheel. Throughout the following chapters, we will break down each segment to accurately depict how to grow into an elite leader.

Leaders must be able to demonstrate each leadership attribute at all times. These characteristics make up the inner circle of the Wheel. There is no attribute on the Leadership Wheel greater than any other in order to complete the Wheel.

Leaders know that no matter how well things are going, you can always expect a bump in the road. They anticipate the bumps before a manager even sees them coming as they use these attributes to navigate their team safely. To help illustrate these

"Meet Cartoon Jon.
He'll be joining us on our travels."

leadership traits, I scheduled the beginning of my trip with chaos in my travels. Since I'd planned my bumps, I knew they were on the horizon but wasn't sure when or how they would occur.

For the beginning of my trip, I will not be traveling in my comfort zone. I enjoy landing in one destination and making it my home for an extended period of time. Traveling is a lot of work when you continually move and are in unchartered waters. I find when you switch locations too often it can be more stressful than fun.

Regardless of what I enjoy, chaos is scheduled for the first twelve days of my trip. During this time, I will be visiting Iceland, Sweden, Finland, Estonia, Latvia, and finally, Cyprus, the island where I wrote my first book. I am delaying my family search as I believe there is an opportunity for a leadership interview in Cyprus. Due to the remoteness of this location, it is considerably less expensive with a stopover in a major European city.

Leaders Plan and React

Life and business happen in a similar fashion. Anyone can manage a top team that never has a bad month, sick day or needs assistance. Imagine how easy life would be if we never got ill, had a broken heart or lost a loved one. Take it a step further and imagine you won

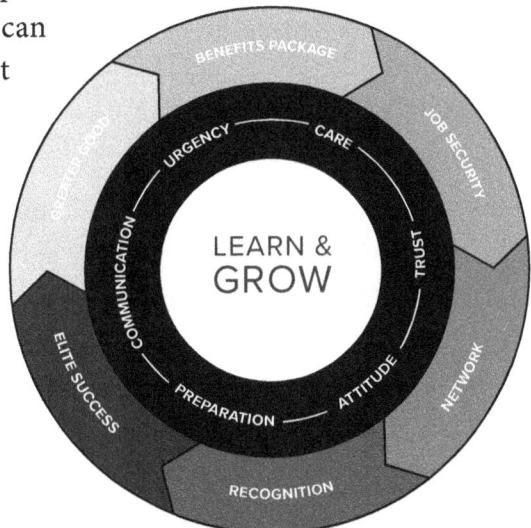

all your athletic events, got perfect grades and consistently got the promotion.

This isn't life nor is it business for the most elite leader. Leaders find the best possible solution for whatever circumstance they are in, and they are not slow to react. This does not mean they hurry to an end result. Leaders are decisive with confidence through testing, research and past knowledge to choose the best path to lead their people.

I was determined to lead myself in the best possible direction through my own bumps and hurdles. And to add an additional element of challenge to the voyage, I'd be filming my own interviews and photographing the trip to help bring the stories to life for the reader. This meant besides writing a book, I would add cameraman and video editor positions to my already busy schedule. *Go to GrassIsBrowner.com or search Grass Is Browner on Instagram, Twitter, and Facebook to find pictures and videos from my travel.*

I have three cameras, a GoPro and only myself to operate everything. If there is a picture or video taken on my travels, it will be taken with a tripod or a sales pitch to someone walking by. The camera equipment, lights and packing for the long term have resulted in two heavy suitcases and a backpack. My work out is scheduled for my travels every time I move locations due to my luggage.

I'm in an Uber—leaving my home in San Diego, California—on the way to the train, which will bring me to Los Angeles. A bus will follow to bring me to the airport for my 9:50 p.m. flight out of LAX. It isn't long before I am waiting at my gate to head to Stockholm, Sweden as the major European city on my way to Cyprus. But my first stop is Iceland as I'd found a flight with a seventeen-hour layover in Keflavik.

This seems like a good start to provide me with some chaos. If I am diligent with my plans in Iceland, I'll be able to do and see a lot in a short amount of time, which is imperative since I only plan to spend a total of seventeen hours in the country. I am going to catch as much sleep as I can during this nine-hour flight.

Icelandic Adventures

I'm refreshed as I wake up to a smooth landing in Keflavik. I begin my Icelandic adventure on a bus ride into the capital, Reykjavik. While touring around their busy streets, I spot the famous Iceland hot dogs. I was skeptical, but I will admit I ate three. So, I guess you could say they were quite good.

With a new energy from all the hotdogs, I head to Puffin Island, which is named due to the large population of puffins calling the island home. It is fascinating as the land and ocean surrounding the island are covered with these birds everywhere the eye can see.

I make my way to Iceland's Blue Lagoon, which is a well-known hot spring. The Blue Lagoon provides me with a necessary bath after my long flight and adventures. I am really enjoying the relaxation, and suddenly, it's 11 p.m. Somehow, there is a tremendous amount of daylight for it being so late.

I continue onward. I can't believe it, but I now have more time to see new areas. The sun, strangely, never set on me. While the moon has come out, I still have enough daylight to view more places. Apparently, I've come to Iceland during the time of the midnight sun, which provides nearly twenty-four hours of daylight.

It has been an amazing day, and I've accomplished more on a layover than others may have achieved during a long weekend. In order to do so, I needed the sun. Had I been here in the winter, this would have been a different experience—their shortest day provides only four hours of daylight.

I am standing in front of the ocean at almost 1 a.m., and decide to shoot my first video of the trip. Looking at a sunset, I am still able to see all around me. If there is one thing I needed today, it's daylight. I needed the sun, and the sun came through.

1st Attribute: Care

It's an unusual way to illustrate our first attribute of leadership. But it's important to note leaders are there when you need them

"Leaders are there when you need them."

because they care. It doesn't mean they are there 24/7. Remember, the winters in Iceland don't see a lot of sun. The daylight is cut down to a short time period. But when I needed the sun most, the sun came through in brilliant fashion.

This analogy of the sun in Iceland illustrates leaders know when they're needed and make sure they are there for their people during those times. Leaders passionately care about growing their team as individuals and people. It's why a leader would never miss a moment where their representative needs something for their career.

Care can and should be further demonstrated through the recognition of achievements, employee anniversaries, birthdays and holidays. But a higher level of care is reached when there is a personal connection to the individuals on your team and their careers. Leaders take the time to learn about their employee's significant others, personal interests and life outside of the office.

We will see this concept throughout the rest of the book in various forms. Therefore, if you do not care about your people, you should not be in a leadership position. Caring is an essential characteristic for a leader in relation to the individuals on your team. If the leader does not care about their employee's careers, these individuals will look elsewhere for someone who does.

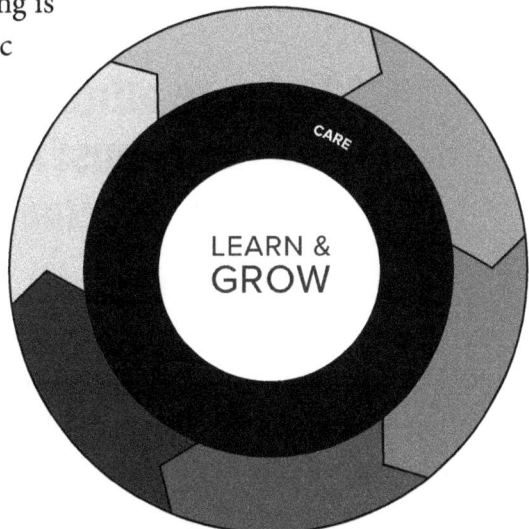

CARE

LEARN &
GROW

Intellectual Honesty

I conducted my first interview for this book with Bob Carr prior to my flight to Iceland. Travels for his new company, Beyond, lead him to San Diego. As a result, this meeting occurred right before leaving my hometown.

Carr founded Heartland Payment Systems, grew it into a Fortune 1000 company, and sold it for 4.3 billion dollars. He was also appointed by President Obama in 2016 to a key White House post on the National Infrastructure Advisory Council. Despite being in a position where most people would settle into fancy dinners, rare wine and extended travel, Carr was going full speed as he'd launched another company.

Leadership is a position where your why is as equally important as your talent. People follow those with a why they can trust. I wanted to find out why Carr was still driven and discuss his own outlook on leadership.

When asked what characteristic had impacted his career the most, Carr quickly responded.

"The core attribute I have that has been most important to me is intellectual honesty."

It was an interesting response as top leaders like to discuss their Emotional Intelligence (EI) to address this topic. This response was, however, not about reading other people, but reading himself. He committed to being honest with himself, his employees and his customers throughout his entire career.

Carr's honesty built followers. "I am regarded as an authentic person. What you see is what you get. And when you can live that through the ups and downs of life, people trust you." Carr wasn't bragging. His honesty and care for other people compelled him to tell the truth, and he was simply sharing how people responded to him and his practice of intellectual honesty.

The number of people coming into his new company was remarkable by anyone's standards. His new company, Beyond, was growing fast. He attributed each individual joining the team from a previous relationship due to his trusted leadership.

It was amazing to hear the drive of this man who didn't need to work, so I pried for an answer as to what was driving him. Carr was blunt. "I did very well with the sale of Heartland. I looked at thirty-five million-dollar yachts, and I looked at nice apartments on Fifth Avenue. But I just love helping kids that wouldn't otherwise go to college."

Carr was talking about his charity, The Give Something Back Foundation. "I can't think of a better way to use my money than to help these kids." His foundation was built to provide mentors and scholarships to help Pell Grant students go to college and graduate in four years, debt-free. (*You can learn more at www.giveback.ngo*)

Carr defended himself well with his sincerity for wanting to help these kids and his employees. "So, why start another company. Because we did it the first time pretty successfully. This time around I'd like to do it without venture capital money and have a business that's 100% employee owned. We're going to make a lot of money and it's going to go to the foundation. Because I'm donating my ownership to the foundation."

I was impressed, but the irony was Carr wasn't being boastful about what he was doing. He took an opposite stance. "I'm very selfish, because I'm doing what I love to do."

Of course, I made him expand as selfish seemed like the wrong way to describe his ambitions. "It's selfish because I'm taking care of my needs. My needs are to do things that make me feel good. And this is what does it for me."

2nd Attribute: Trust

Leaders are required to care about their people. If you are only looking to benefit yourself through a leadership position, you will never be a leader. Leaders understand by appreciating and caring for their people, they will respond in kind. Carr illustrated his belief that it is impossible to care for your people, company or customers if you are not honest with them. Trust, therefore, becomes the second attribute required of a leader.

If you work for Bob Carr, you are guaranteed to be working for someone you can trust. His theme was wanting to help his employees, the kids through his foundation, and doing the right thing by being honest. This is a man who demonstrated trusting and caring attributes throughout his interview.

Carr's why was something others would get behind. There was added trust to follow Carr for his bigger mission over simply growing profits for a company. He was growing profits for his foundation to help kids go to college. His previous experience told his story of continually providing learning and growth. He was well known for promoting from within and advancing those within his company by encouraging individuals to soar to new heights they did not know were possible.

Trust does not solely mean being honest with your team. Managers can be trusted, but they are often looking for immediate gratification. To the opposite, leaders do right by their people and work towards the long haul. Elite teams take time, dedication, and trust in the leader to coach the team in the right direction. This is the trust needed to accomplish this core attribute of leadership.

Caring and trust are both core components necessary to create an environment of learning and growth. While Carr is often seen as a compassionate leader, this is not a requirement for the trust or care of one's team as this can be shown quite different across the diversity of leaders. Some of the most successful leaders are regarded as rude, tough or arrogant. The theme on trust and caring has direct relation to each individual's career. Leaders help people grow their careers and this demonstrates caring for each of these individuals as they do so. This means an elite leader could be a jerk, but they create an environment of results where employees trust they will learn, grow and make more money as they advance their careers.

Define your Mission

People will follow the why as much as they follow the leader. This doesn't mean you need to change your company's model to give a chunk of your profits to charity. It

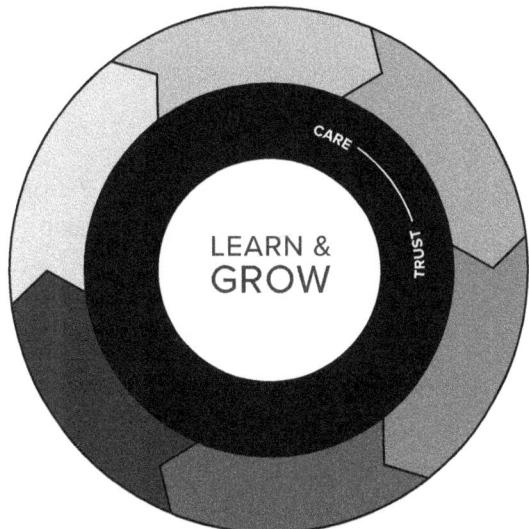

means your team needs to understand their purpose. What are they chasing and why are they chasing it?

Each leader should clearly define the mission statement of their sales team. This should be different than your company's mission statement as it must be combined with your team goal. It should speak to your team and create a motivational environment to chase the mission collectively as a team. In a sales environment, it should be geared towards sales. A good example of this would be:

"We will be the #1 team this year and do so with honesty, integrity and dedication to providing our customers with the best service."

The goal can be associated with some type of team reward upon accomplishment. But ultimately, an environment must be created where the goal evolves to accomplishing the mission itself. Any reward should simply be a celebration of the accomplishment.

In order to create a mission statement for your sales team, you'll want to have three things present in your one sentence goal and mission statement.

1. A specific measurement of success. (Team Goal)

2. A timeline for the measurement. (Team Goal)

3. A greater meaning behind what you're looking to accomplish. (Team Mission)

Once again, a sales team's mission statement needs to be different than a company's vision. While Carr's vision for his company can fixate on the goal of growing the company to help kids go to college and give back to the employees, a sales team is driven by sales. Although intrinsically valuable, a sales team cannot function by only doing community service and giving back to others.

A sales team still needs sales—hence, why the team goal must be present. With established and accomplished sales goals, the fulfillment aspect of what the team would like to accomplish through their mission will grow with the success of the team. Initially, a team's mission may simply be acting with intellectual honesty to achieve their goal. This is a great mission! We'll learn later on how an elite sales team can achieve a greater good for the company.

Take time to think about your team's goal and mission statement and then come back to the end of this chapter to clearly define it in the space below. Please make sure you include all three items needed for a successful statement. This will drive your team forward as you continue to brand your vision of growing an elite team. You'll know you have a successful mission statement when the team starts quoting it without your direction.

Team Goal and Mission Statement:

_____

_____

_____

_____

_____

2

King of Snoresville

I am back at the airport with time to spare for my flight to Stockholm. I keep thinking about how my time in Iceland went smoother than I could have imagined. Even with the adrenaline of the trip being off to a good start, exhaustion is taking over after my seventeen hours of adventure in Iceland.

Finally, I'm on the plane in my window seat with two gentlemen sitting next to me. They look tired as well. I am relieved to not be stuck next to someone who wants to chat the entire flight.

As the plane is taking off, I snap a couple pictures of Iceland's interesting landscape. The plane is settling above the clouds, and I no longer need nor want the sun. I reach for my sleep mask to block out the light and get some rest. As I reach into my backpack, the passenger in the middle seat starts to snore. And the passenger in the aisle is out cold. I can hear him snoring as well. No big deal. Planes are loud, and I am exhausted.

With my sleep mask on, I attempt to relax myself into a slumber—a nap is necessary in order to survive my travels once I get to Stockholm. As I start to doze off, I hit my first bump in the road—a loud bump. In fact, it seems to be getting louder by the minute. I truly believe if there was a snoring contest for volume, the man sitting next to me would win.

I am sleep deprived but wide awake and fascinated. I had expected bumps in the road, but I never expected to meet the King of Snoresville on my flight. I'm contemplating recording the whole ordeal. I pull out my iPhone to take a selfie video next to the roar of King Snore, but stop myself. I don't want to be disrespectful to the person next to me.

The preparation for my travels did not include earplugs, so I won't be falling asleep anytime soon. I am too tired to keep writing and want to avoid typing anything I would be embarrassed to read the next day. I know this bump in the road will be causing me problems in the hours to come.

On the four-hour flight to Stockholm, I listen to the encore of the snoring concert over and over again. I decide to be thankful I'm wide-awake and can take a few pictures flying into Stockholm. I'm anxious to get off the plane and grab a large coffee to power through my next excursion.

My next destination was again designed to allow chaos to ensue during my initial travels. Instead of waiting for an immediate flight from Sweden to Cyprus; I am taking a cruise ship to two other countries and back prior to my flight to the island. Coffee in hand and luggage accounted for, I confidently walk out of the airport in search of my bus into the center of the city. I already have my bus ticket, so I merely need to locate my transportation.

With no energy to celebrate this victory of foreign travel, I halfheartedly slump into the first open seat on the bus. I somewhat doze off as my head drops and continually hits the seat in front of me.

I awake to a brisk stop and a final head butt on my route to the bus station. Looking like a zombie, I exit the bus and haul my luggage with plenty of time to figure out how to get to my cruise ship headed to Helsinki, Finland.

Learning I have an hour until my next bus, I walk to the first food service I can find inside the bus station to replenish. I now have my large checked bag, my carry-on suitcase and my heavy backpack as my exercise for the day. Not wanting to leave my luggage behind for someone to take, I climb this mountain of Stockholm with it in tow and place my order: sandwich, yogurt, coffee, and a water.

The coffee will be ready in a minute. The man at the counter hands me the sandwich, water, and yogurt on a tray.

"Can I get some mustard?" I ask.

He is staring back at me as if he doesn't understand. I repeat my request for mustard, and he points to the restroom.

"Thank you." I am too tired to figure out how to explain this condiment, and I need to sit down. I now know where the bathroom is, so I'll take that as a win.

I look at the tray. I look at my two rolling suitcases. I even give a head turn to my heavy backpack, contemplating how to get everything over to the nearest table twenty-five feet away.

I pause, thinking I should ask for help, but know I would just end up with a map to the restroom. I attempt to roll the two suitcases with one hand as I balance everything else on the tray. For my first three steps, this is the right choice. But with the crash of the sandwich plate on the fourth step, I learn otherwise. The clang of the plate and splatter of the yogurt container results in thirty people staring at me. Thankfully, I catch the sandwich with my arm against my leg, and the water bottle is still good, so I haven't completely ruined my meal.

"New." The man behind the counter keeps repeating while trying to take my sandwich.

"I don't want a new sandwich. It's okay; it didn't hit the ground. I caught it."

Maybe he thinks I'm still talking about the restroom because he just keeps repeating "new."

"Leaders anticipate bumps in the road."

I give up and hand over my squashed sandwich. I roll my suitcases to the nearest table as he brings me my food.

"Thank you." I say at least five times. This he understands.

3rd Attribute: Attitude

In leadership and in life, we all face adversity. Your attitude will be a determining factor of your success. As a leader, your attitude will not only determine your success, but it will factor into the performance of your team. Our third attribute required for leaders is a positive attitude.

It's easy to have an awesome attitude when you are well rested and everything goes as planned. But your team will look to you when they question their own esteem. Individuals on your team will lose out on a big sale. They will spend an entire day telemarketing and not set a single appointment. They may struggle to learn product knowledge. Your job is to have a positive attitude in these situations and be a cheerleader for them to do the same. Attitude becomes our third characteristic along with trust and care as core attributes of leadership.

In my instance, I want to eat my food and fall asleep at the restaurant. But nothing about my current situation is traumatic. I am a few hours from getting on the cruise boat to

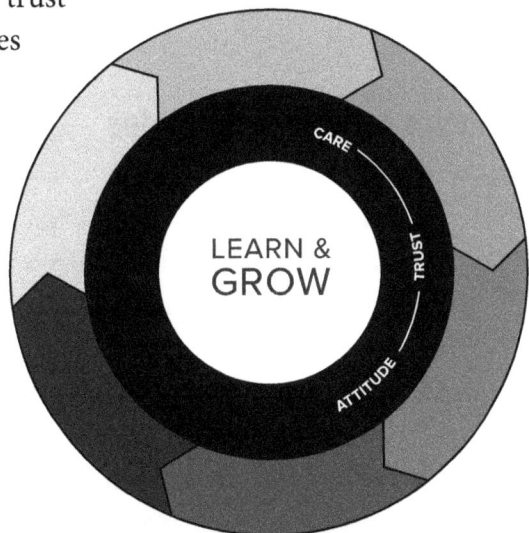

Helsinki. I know I can drink my coffee and stay awake until I board the ship. Then I will immediately take a nap for my own safety and sanity. I have my plan, and I am happy about it. Everything is still working out despite what feels like extenuating circumstances.

It's important everyone stay positive, but even more so in leadership positions. No one is motivated to learn or grow by a pessimistic leader. Some people are able to create motivation on their own, but you don't get to take credit for their awesome attitude. Leaders are required to contribute to each individual's drive, esteem and success.

Because each person is motivated differently, it's important you understand the members of your team and what drives them. Knowing how to properly motivate and coach your people builds positivity into your team. It's not your attitude speaking to the sales prospects, so you must remember your sales reps' attitudes will define the success of your team. Leaders utilize emotional intelligence (EI) to cue them in on personality traits and what motivates their people. But there are simpler ways to find out what drives the members of your team. Ask them.

Hire Awesome Attitudes

As a best practice, you'll want to find out how someone wants to be coached and what drives them prior to starting the position. This will provide insight on the kind of environment they deem positive and assist you in keeping them motivated and driven. For anyone you hire, the following three interview questions will be advantageous for your relationship with your new hire and insight on their attitude.

1. How do you like to be coached?

2. What motivates you to push yourself further?

3. If you aren't achieving the minimum results, how do you prefer to be managed?

Expectations are crucial. Your relationship with the employee starts on their first interview, it does not start on their first day. You must be open and honest about what the job is and set expectations of the position. Do not inflate someone's expectations on the income. You should provide them with details of what someone will make at quota and what top sales professionals are making within the company. It is important you know what the average income is of a first-year representative and communicate this along with detailing all of the benefits clearly.

You are searching for a candidate who is excited about the compensation, benefits and the opportunity with appropriate expectations. These questions will give insight to your new hire's attitude. No leader would willingly hire a bad attitude as it can lower production for the entire team.

Navigating through the questions above provides an agreed upon method for your relationship and allows you to set expectations on an employee's attitude should you move forward with working together. This gives you the opportunity, prior to them starting, to outline policies, your involvement and what they can expect from you as a leader. This should take place despite any unusual requests they might have on how they want to be managed. It is your job to be honest and direct. It is not your job to adhere to demands which go against company structure or team dynamics.

When problems occur, you can reference this conversation from their interview. You should re-open the dialogue to discuss the necessity of achieving their goals for their own income and the team. Ultimately, leaders are consistently looking to grow performance and knowledge for their team member's own good. Your consistency on what you are doing and your openness to each person will have each member of the team working with you positively to achieve success.

Leaders Are Professors

Leaders know when to adapt their leadership methods or change course in order to push results forward. This allows a leader to get the most out of their people. No one can operate at their peak level without navigating new terrain. This in and of itself creates a learning environment.

In order to instruct, leaders must strive to continually grow their own knowledge. Leaders must practice *ABL –always be learning.* If you read my first book, you are familiar with this concept. It doesn't matter if you hold a sales or leadership position, it is important everyone continuously learn throughout their careers. Those learning and growing consistently site greater employee satisfaction than individuals stagnant in their positions. Learning is therefore essential for a positive attitude to form on the team.

By a leader continuing to learn, they place themselves in a position where they are prepared to teach; they share new and updated knowledge with their team and peers to increase positivity around them. You will never be considered a leader if you do not foster an environment of learning and growth. *ABT* becomes part of your expected behavior from your team.

ABT – always be teaching.

Following this practice will provide the largest contribution a leader can make towards the attitudes of the individuals on their team.

Do not singularly rely on your future hire's response for insight on their attitude. In an interview, most people will provide the answer you want to hear. They are selling you on giving them the job.

Always do reference checks. But throw out your standard set of questions. You should understand even an average candidate will have at least three people to tell you they're great. Obviously, let the reference articulate this sentiment for good measure. But you should use the reference check for greater insight on how your future employee needs to be coached. Ask the following three questions to former managers during the phone call:

1. How does this person prefer to be coached and how do they need to be coached?

2. What does this person need from their manager to be pushed to greater results?

3. If this person isn't achieving results, what is the best way to manage them?

These questions should look similar to what you asked your candidate. Most times, you'll find better insight from the previous manager. You may even smoke out a bad attitude prior to hiring one on your team. A track record of negativity should be avoided at all costs. Not only will it affect the success of your new hire, but bad attitudes are contagious. They will affect your team's attitude and even your own.

Thank each reference check you speak with and connect to them on LinkedIn. Leaders surround themselves with a large network. These contacts can create positive reinforcement to your relationship with your future employee along with providing referrals to new candidates. Leaders are well-connected and never miss a networking opportunity to benefit their team.

New Heights

Your job as a leader is to create a positive environment and a motivational culture. In order to do so, your attitude must be willing to absorb the bumps in the road for your team. You are the filter for your team; you must remove the obstacles in order for your team to concentrate positively on their daily tasks.

Leaders collaborate with their individuals to help them achieve a level of success they never thought possible. This will occur because each team member has prepared a business plan to follow. And people excitedly chase what they create. Don't tell your sales reps how to achieve their goals. Success can be achieved in various ways. While there are minimum expectations at every company, each person can get to those requirements differently.

We'll discuss creating an initial business plan in greater detail in our next chapter. Right now, the most important part of creating the plan is the positivity and excitement surrounded by it from you and your sales individual. A positive attitude is hard to teach, so it's crucial to interview for this as an intangible. You can't control a stranger snoring next to you for an entire flight, but you can control how you respond. Hire reps who are not derailed by the inevitable noise.

Control Your Response

My grandfather, Ken Markwardt, instructs wisdom through all of life's events. "It's mind over matter, Jon. It's all in your head." He believes this mantra applies to everything in life.

Whatever you believe, you can achieve. He even believes this applies to something as trivial as a common cold. If you believe you are sick, you are sick. You will stay in bed all day. You will feel sorry for yourself. You won't be productive. And you will wait for the cold to subside before you adjust your attitude and go about your regular day.

Every time I've seen my grandfather with a cold, I ask him how he is feeling. And every time, he responds the same. "I'm fine. It's just a little cold. It doesn't bother me."

This lesson isn't about getting sick. Of course, everyone gets sick. But don't let it affect your attitude. Stay moving. Stay busy. My grandfather achieved great things in the business world through his positivity. Everyone could count on him to be working full speed ahead despite there being a bump in the road. And everyone knew the optimal result would come to fruition despite any detours taken. People reporting to my grandfather never felt the enormity of a bump in the road, because it was just a little bump.

My grandfather's own search into our family tree had too many bumps for him to find the answers he searched for. The relatives he learned of sent correspondence written in German, Russian and Polish, all containing little knowledge of his father's history.

While it had been over ten years since my grandfather last received a letter from Poland, I wasn't deterred from making this voyage. My grandpa had taught me to minimize negativity in my life. I was on a voyage with the assistance of technology for translating communication and a high sense of urgency to find the answers my grandfather never found.

Think about the leaders you've worked for who minimize the bumps. You may not even know when problems occur under great leadership. Now think about the managers who turn the bumps into mountains. The consequences for responding one way or the other are severe and are all about the attitude and message you send to your team.

As a leader, it is your job to make sure your team knows everything is fine. Half the battle of minimizing the bump is the recognition of the problem. Acknowledging the issue allows you to formulate a plan. And finding a solution will navigate your team in the right direction to keep them moving. You do not want your team to take the bump and your negative attitude as an excuse to curl up in bed and snore.

Prior to moving on to the next chapter, list the three biggest bumps you currently have or will face on your team.

1. _____
   _____

2. _____
   _____

3. _____
   _____

3

Look in the Mirror

The boat's horn jumps me awake from my seated nap in the cruise ship's boarding area. I am anxious to get to my room and lie down for a few minutes. I am one of the first on board and have almost an hour before departure. Despite my desperation to sleep, I know I can't go to sleep for the entire night at three in the afternoon. It's important to adapt to the time change for me to enjoy Finland, so I take a quick nap.

Refreshed from my nap, I watch our boat travel out of Stockholm from the top deck. The route to Finland is gorgeous. I can't believe the number of islands and small islets as we travel. Some of these small islands were only large enough for a flock of birds to take a rest during their own travels at sea.

As the boat advances in route, I am surprised but not entirely shocked to learn Finland is the home of 179,000 islands. No wonder the view is so incredible heading to the port of Helsinki.

Don't Delay Success

I wrote my first book to fulfill an ambition I had for years. I realized this goal ten times over with positive feedback from colleagues, friends and people I've never met. However, it is rare that a first-time author achieves the monetary success necessary to, confidently, pursue such a career fulltime.

My path is no different; my first book sold numerous copies, but it was not harnessing enough income to support my current lifestyle. Regardless, I received a strong push to continue pursuing my dream six days after my first book launched. I got word one of my closest friends, Steve Junor, had a glioblastoma on his spinal cord. His diagnosis is a constant and acute reminder that life is short, and it's important to follow your dreams now. The next day, I made the decision to become an author and speaker full-time.

A decision and action are two different things. And, in the past, my action was moving slowly. Steve's glioblastoma, on the other hand, was unfortunately not; we watched his physical health deteriorate rapidly during the first six months post his diagnosis. The pressure of the tumor on his spinal cord caused Steve to limp, and eventually required the use of a cane. Then came the walker, and finally, a wheel chair became necessary to get around.

While his wedding plans were abruptly called off, they were at equal speed brought back on. Steve had quickly embraced his own action plan of living life in the now and enjoying the moment. The wedding occurred less than two months after the diagnosis and was a blast for everyone in attendance.

Mirror Neurons

I watched my close friend get married, travel every weekend, and embrace life more than he'd ever done before. And it wasn't a mirage when you spoke with him. He was truly enjoying his life, and it was infectious to the people around him.

A diagnosis like this turns the patient into a leader. However the individual chooses to respond, the family and friends will mirror. Embrace and enjoy life, the surrounding family and friends do likewise. How could they not? It's easy to mirror smiles, laughter and fun. It is often amplified from the mirror neurons in our bodies.

Mirror neurons fire off in your body when you see an action performed by another. The neurons copy the behavior of the other person almost as though the person observing was the one creating the action. From psychological studies, it is believed these neurons assist humans in our communication, understanding and ability to acquire new skills.

The contagiousness of laughter or a smile is a fun example. When everyone is laughing, you may find yourself joining in despite not understanding the joke. And it can be a rather entertaining social experiment. You can google laughing on a subway to find a few humorous videos. They may even set off your own mirror neurons as you join in on the laughter.

Regardless of the science behind it, Steve did not create a dark cloud over his head. He was prepared to embrace life and effectively have his surrounding friends and family do the same. And that's exactly what occurred. While the diagnosis is serious and scary for everyone involved, I've consistently enjoyed my time with him post-diagnosis. He leads me to laugh, smile and embrace the moment through his attitude on life.

On a weekend visit, we'd had our own fun filming a second commercial for my first book. The commercials were comedic distractions with Steve playing the star role in both videos. It was important to embrace these random activities to still have our normal fun. You can see his Christmas and Valentine's Day commercials with his wife, Leslie, as the co-star at GrassIsBrowner.com/press.

Steve and his wife live in Grover Beach, which is about five hours north of my home in San Diego. Right before I left, Steve informed me. "I've never lived more in my life than when I found out I was dying." After this conversation, my own words started working toward action. I replayed our conversation the entire way back to San Diego. I didn't listen to the radio. I simply drove in silence and thought about what he said.

I didn't need my own diagnosis to embrace life and stand strong in my decision to seize the day. Steve pushed me to pursue my dreams now. I started to plan how I could make a transition in my own life and career.

Four months later, I left my corporate position in leadership. I had my initial travel set to fly to Cyprus through Stockholm, prior to searching for my family roots in Germany and Poland. When I detailed my travel plans to Steve, he offered to reach out to a friend in Finland. He was confident she would show me around or have a friend play tour guide if she wasn't in town.

This is why my low on sleep body is looking out at these beautiful islands as I travel from Stockholm to Helsinki. Steve's friend, Mia, is not in town, but she has arranged for me to play Finnish baseball with her women's team, and her friend, Liisa, is going to take me around the city as well.

4th Attribute: Preparation

My first day in Finland is strategically planned by Liisa, even though she won't actually be with me. She sent an itinerary to me, detailing every hour I will be in Helsinki during my three-day trip. Everything is orchestrated for me to have an amazing time and meet her on day two.

The first day is the most important day of anyone's career. It is crucial due to one question everyone's friends and family will ask: "How was your first day?" In one day, you will create a culture of question or excitement surrounding this person's new job. It is obvious which one you are trying to create.

Preparation is the key to a successful first day. You, as the leader, must be ready. Let the new hire know your plan before they show up. You'll want them confident and excited about their first day. I am looking forward to my Finland plans and there isn't even anyone to greet me. Liisa made me comfortable through her detailed instructions and preparation.

Preparation is our fourth leadership attribute. Leaders are prepared each day for every situation. Without preparing for your employees and new hire, it is impossible to have any type of learning environment in place to benefit the growth of the individuals you lead.

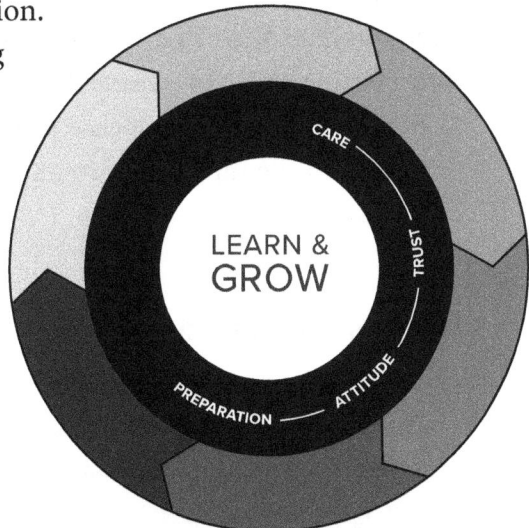

CARE

LEARN &
GROW

TRUST

PREPARATION — ATTITUDE

Lunch is the Most Important Meal of the Day

If you are in an office, you should have a welcome sign at your new hire's desk autographed by everyone on the team. Their desk should be clean and have new office supplies. Your first job will be to tour them around the facility and introduce them to people they need to know. And don't forget to show them where the bathroom is.

You'll want to make sure the first day is filled with education along with setting expectations on how they will be successful in the role. There is never a more important time to do a business plan than on someone's first day. But equally as important will be your lunch outing to get to know each other personally.

The lunch allows you to share your personal care for fostering their success in the company. A strong start to your relationship will have the energy and care you provide for your new hire mirrored with their actions from day one. Use the mirror neurons to your advantage.

While they may not completely understand how to be successful in the organization, they should have greater direction after their first day. This requires them to go home with a business plan to achieve the success they are shooting for. As discussed earlier, appropriate expectations should have been discussed in the interview process, so there are no surprises on day one.

Telemarketing Math

Sales is math, and no one gets to decide on the variables that effect the equation. There are different items to calculate for whatever you are looking to accomplish. If you close at 33% and don't get the sale on your appointment, you simply need to go on two more appointments to generate a sale. Obviously, the results must be taken over a larger period of time to be accurate. But the math is the same for every industry and sales position, so it is crucial you are prepared to know the math on your own team. A leader must understand their numbers in order to prepare realistic business plans and goals with their sales reps.

Likewise, telemarketing can get tough when someone yells at you over the phone. But this is math again. It takes a certain number of dials to reach a decision-maker who is able to set an appointment with you. You will close for an appointment at a certain percentage over the phone. And you will close these future meetings for a sale at a specific closing ratio. Knowing all of this, you can calculate the number of dials it will take to get a sale. If someone hangs up on you, they saved you time; you are getting closer to the next dial which will lead to your next sale.

While working for a Fortune 1000 company, I diligently monitored this dialing equation. It was typically skewed to the negative for newer representatives. But it was important for them to learn where they needed to take their telemarketing skills to hit the appropriate averages. I was able to calculate with my senior representatives that they would make twenty-seven dials an hour. Seven of these dials were decision-makers who answered and could set an appointment. Every dial counted, and a voicemail was left on every phone call not answered. On average, we would close for an appointment at 15%, or one appointment for every seven decision-makers we spoke with.

The established sales professional is important to this equation. My newer representatives or those struggling would typically take two to three hours to set one appointment.

Anything over two hours would provide math equating to not making enough dials, not getting enough contacts from a poor list, or struggling with their phone skills as they weren't able to set an appointment.

These appointments were typically a little colder and thus my tenured professionals would close at a high of 20%. If you are averaging one appointment per hour and close these meetings at 20%, it would take you five hours of telemarketing to get one sale.

5 Appointments x 20% Closing Ratio = 1 Sale

27 Dials per Hour x 5 Hours = 135 Dials to generate 1 Sale

$$\frac{B+X}{F^X} + \sqrt{\frac{B+F\overset{X}{\infty}}{FB}} = FUN$$

"Numbers make sales fun!"

Have Fun!

Understanding the math takes the emotion and frustration out of telemarketing. You can work on word tracks, find a better list, or keep dialing. I'm proud to share a story of one of my own telemarketing blunders for comedic relief when someone is struggling. I encourage you to do the same. Learn to celebrate these stories and laugh—they get you to that next, dreaded dial and lead to your next sale.

For me, I believe telemarketing is a game. I play it like some people play the lottery. I prefer telemarketing because the odds of winning are substantially higher. Telemarketing gives you an opportunity to skew the numbers. If I can set my appointments quicker, I can stop telemarketing. The equation for your next sale has nothing to do with hours. It has everything to do with the appointments set as seen in the first equation above.

Provide an environment for your representatives to play. Prepare telemarketing contests, challenges and team dialing. On the other end of the phone, the prospect can hear your enthusiasm and will know if you are proud of your product. Provide your team with an environment where they smile and dial.

Your voice sounds different when you smile, and this can be heard on the phone. This is not a psychological concept. It is physiological. When you smile, the soft palate at the back of your mouth raises, thus changing your vocals. The sound becomes more fluid as your mouth opens wider from the simple exercise of smiling.

Make sure your new representative understands the telemarketing equation and the number of dials required as a necessary part of the position. Break down the math for this individual and add it to their business plan as they grow their pipeline, knowledge and network. By understanding the math, we can all be happier to get to the next dial after a rude encounter. And if your representatives are happy, the prospects will hear them smiling.

Prepare a Business Plan

Telemarketing is a necessary part of the business plan, but it's often the last thing a sales professional wants to do. Let them put it in. And they will if you've made the appropriate illustration as to why it's vital. While there may be mandatory telemarketing time for all, you want them to be motivated for it to achieve their income objective.

Goals are calculated with four standard variables. And you'll want to walk them through these levers to achieve their target income. Here are the four components of calculating their sales goal:

1. **Time:** This is typically measured in weeks of the year. If an employee takes two weeks of vacation, you have fifty total weeks. Monthly business plans will typically be done with four weeks.

2. **Closing Ratio:** Total Sales divided by Total Appointments during a set time period. This gives you a percentage for the number of appointments you need to get a sale.

3. **Revenue Per Unit:** While some companies measure this in Profit or Margin Per Unit, the more common measurement is the annualized revenue for the new account. Calculate this by dividing the individual's

total revenue over a set time period by the number of units sold.

4. **Appointments Per Week:** This measurement should be done with new appointments. Each company has a different policy as to when a follow-up meeting will count. If your company does not, you must establish this for your team in order to provide greater accuracy to the business plan.

With these variables, you are able to calculate sales goals factually to get someone where they want to be financially. With someone new, preparation is required by the leader to know the averages of those coming into the organization to set realistic expectations. You can share what the top representatives are doing during this exercise so your new hire can see how moving the levers up or down will affect their success.

The number you are looking to find is the number of appointments per week. You'll compare this to their previous average to decide if their goal is realistic for someone beyond their first day. For a new person, you should be navigating them above the minimum activity required. They are new and should be putting in the extra effort. It will be necessary as they won't be fully knowledgeable on the product at the beginning of their career or have an established pipeline.

Stretch Goal

If the stretch goal appears unrealistic for the appointments per week, you'll need to collaborate with the sales representative on how to increase their closing ratio, revenue per unit, appointments per week or possibly all three. I'll provide a quick example here. If you have a representative with an annual goal of $500,000 in revenue, how many appointments do they need to go on each week with a 40% closing ratio, $5000 revenue per unit average, and a plan of two weeks of vacation for the year?

$$40\% \times \$5000 \times 50 \times \underline{\hspace{2cm}} = \$500,000$$

(Closing Ratio) x (Revenue Per Unit) x (Weeks Worked) x (Appointments Per Week) = Annualized Goal

You will divide the three numbers on the left by the goal number on the right to get the necessary appointments per week. $500,000 / 50 / $5000 / .40 = 5 appointments per week

Now, the question becomes how they get to five solid appointments per week. Their previous appointment per week average will help you determine how to create the business plan. If they were averaging four appointments per week, they'll need to get one extra appointment every week to achieve their stretch goal.

You may have noticed I've written stretch goal multiple times. Leaders push their individuals to new heights. While you don't want them setting unrealistic goals to become unmotivated, a leader should push the limits on what they can do. In a motivated and supportive culture, you'll find your representatives able to stretch further than they initially believed.

As you formulate the business plan, you should be working towards three action items to support the stretch goal. More than three action items will become a deterrent for the representative to implement everything. Not only that, but it may be unrealistic to hold the individual accountable to what's been agreed upon. Likewise, if you implement less than three, you are not coaching the individual to their full potential.

For established sales professionals, the business plan may be working on achieving their results in less time to push down their total weeks worked. You can calculate the equation in a similar fashion by inputting all of the numbers other than the weeks worked. This can be motivating for a professional seeking a greater work-life balance. Remember, their goal is your goal.

No matter what your rep's ambition, your job is to help them achieve it. Working less is a perfectly acceptable business plan to help drive a tenured representative to their own definition of success. Meanwhile, they will take care of what they need to do for the team and company while growing their own career in the direction they choose.

Make sure you fill out the goal numbers of the business plan and write the three action items the sales rep has agreed on. Once this is accomplished, you will want your employee to sign and date it. Give them a copy and ask them to put it somewhere they will see it each day. Let them know you'll be holding them accountable to this plan during their one-on-one, which we will discuss further in Chapter 11.

If you do not have a standard business plan created for your team, you are able to download a generic one at GrassIsBrowner.com/documents. You'll also find a calculator to assist you on the equation for required appointments per week. As we've learned here, preparation is the key for leaders to build business plans and coach their employees to stretch goals. It is impossible to build any type of plan or advise on any type of goal when you are unprepared to do so.

The bottom line as a leader is this: who you hire and how you onboard them will influence your team's success greater than anything else you do. Proportionately, the first day is crucial to help navigate your new hire in a direction of comfort and excitement. Everything else you do in your role should be working to expand yourself as a leader and the greater good of the individuals of your team and company.

Prior to moving on to the next chapter, you'll want to make sure you are preparing properly for all leadership activities. This core attribute of leaders is necessary for your team meetings, interviews, one-on-one's and entire day-to-day schedule. At the same time, there is no greater time to be prepared than on someone's first day. You must be prepared to navigate your new hire through a business plan with an accurate understanding of the numbers. This person has made a big decision to follow you, so you need to plan for the start of their career.

Create a list of the top ten things you will do on someone's first day to ensure they tell their friends and family they are excited about their new position. The first eight items are filled in for you. Have fun with the remaining two!

1. Prior to their first day, provide them with an outline of what will be accomplished on day one.

2. Have a welcome sign at their clean desk with new supplies.

3. Buy them lunch, and get to know each other on a personal level.

4. Go through a first-year business plan discussing their income objective, levers to achieve their goal and activities necessary to get them there.

5. Roleplay a sales presentation.

6. Make telemarketing calls with them, observing for one hour.

7. Make in-person cold calls together for one hour.

8. Give them a copy of *The Grass Is Browner on the Other Side* (Sales Edition).

   a. You can obviously insert a different copy here, but I'm in sales too! The point is to give them a copy of a book you want them to read. This will establish a culture of learning and growth with your new employee.

9. _____

   _____

10. _____

   _____

4

Finnish Baseball

I am having an amazing first day in Finland following Liisa's itinerary. I am meeting many people who don't speak English, but I am not discouraged. I can't speak Finnish, but I feel like a local. I know what to do, where to go and fun foods to eat. I am grateful for Liisa's preparation to ensure my enjoyable travel.

I am confidently touring myself around Helsinki, but my sleep deprivation is kicking in from the dramatic time change. I've taken many pictures of the city and have found an enjoyable place to eat some local Finnish food. After my delicious meal of salmon soup, I am rejuvenated for my next adventure in navigating myself by bus to my Finnish baseball event.

Comfortable Environment

Considering how tired I am from my travels, there would have been no shame to an unambitious day. Tomorrow is my scheduled time with Liisa, who speaks fluent English. But on my own, I am comfortable in my new environment. Different circumstances would have me going to bed early and not venturing outside of the city to play baseball with strangers. With encouraging text messages from Liisa and instructions to navigate by bus, my day continues onward to my unchartered event.

When you are in a foreign country, it can be uncomfortable when you struggle with basic conversation. Navigating yourself to a remote location is often hard. This could result in foreign travelers opting to stay somewhere comfortable and play on their phones. There are plenty of people in my phone who would respond in English if I reached out.

Do not put yourself in a position where your new hire becomes thrilled to communicate with someone else. This other person will most likely be a recruiter if they find a communication barrier with their new boss. Your top priority whenever you on-board someone is to get them to a point where they are on autopilot and have a trusting relationship with you. This means you must provide them with the tools and education to operate their day in a successful manner on their own. It is your responsibility to provide them with the appropriate education on the product or service, the company and anything they need to be successful within a comfortable work environment. This will get them to a spot where they can navigate the position on their own and call on their trusted leader when needed.

This will often mean showing them what to do as you demonstrate and they watch. You should never make the mistake of assuming your new hire understands all the intricacies of what you are doing. An environment of trust must be in place.

Communication is the number one factor in an employee growing a career at a company.

You will need your new employee to trust that you are providing them with the right direction to follow your instructions. It will be a necessary part of the process for the trust to go both ways. If your new hire does not understand something, you will need to expect they are communicating this to you.

5th Attribute: Communication

Communication is the number one factor in an employee growing a career at a company. Fail to communicate with your new hire, and they will communicate their frustration to someone else. This could result in encouragement to leave the company when an employee faces poor interaction with their manager.

Communication is our fifth core attribute required for leadership. There is no

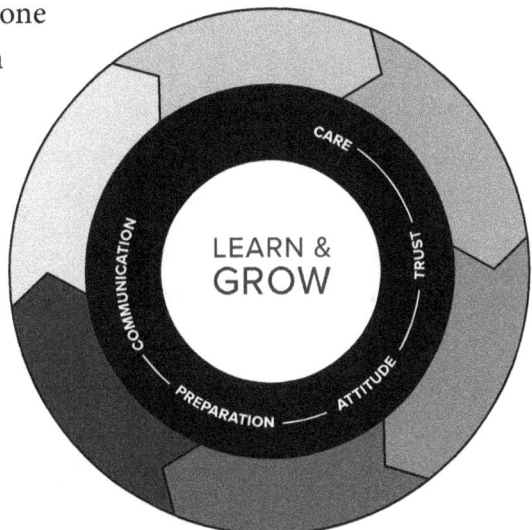

amount of communication too great as your employee develops at your company. For their first ninety days, you should have a daily call or in-person meeting at the beginning and end of each day.

During this meeting, you will work towards your new hire running the agenda. In the morning, they should be sharing their plan for the day and asking you questions to improve the quality of their sales tasks and appointments. At the end of the day is their time to recap and receive insight from their activity to gain company knowledge and process perspective.

If you are prepared for these meetings and don't allow anything to interrupt them, this communication will create a positive environment of caring and trust. You will become their trusted advisor for success in their career as these conversations help your employee secure little wins. As the conversations continue, the wins will grow bigger, and their trust and confidence in their leader will strengthen. This entire process builds toward a point in time when these meetings are no longer necessary as the employee grows their knowledge, sales and success within the company.

Leaders coach their individuals to a point where the leader becomes involved only when the representative needs them. The goal is for the individual to grow into an elite sales representative and leader on the team in their own regard. Both the leader and the individual will enjoy more freedom when learning, growth and advancement occur.

No leader should ever be so arrogant to believe their new hire should learn everything directly from them. There are huge dividends to be made through diversity in their education. Someone else could communicate the same thing you are saying, but it might click with another's coaching. Do your best to involve your team, the training department, the top sales representatives and any other resource at your disposal during someone's onboarding.

The most important part of this integration is getting them welcomed to the entire team. Your team is actively selling and will provide different communication than you do as a leader. Greater credibility and insight often comes from suggestions not made by a direct manager. When you have a team with leaders on it, they will instinctively help coach their teammates in the right direction. This peer communication will formulate an intricate part of your new hire's success and create comradery within the team.

Team Communication

The easiest way to integrate a new hire is by planning a team event. It should be a top priority to have one within the first week of your new hire coming on-board. Two weeks may be more appropriate depending on how in-depth and hands-on your initial training is after their first day. But do your best to plan it right away.

The event could simply be a happy hour. But I would encourage you to have greater interaction through your social outing ranging anywhere from mini-golf to indoor sky-diving to kickball—depending on your budget. The point is an event should not be pendant on an expense account. Leaders know some costs are required to invest in their team. Do not be afraid to spend money on a fun event to strengthen the individuals you manage.

As a tourist in a foreign land, Finnish baseball is my team event to learn a new sport and communicate with locals in a fun environment. My afternoon continues as I successfully find the women's team and baseball field. I am fortunate to be greeted with a few people able to speak English, and they are prepared for my arrival.

"Have you ever played Finnish baseball before?" Three different women greet me with the same question. I am beginning to realize their baseball must be much different from the American baseball I am accustomed to.

It was one of the most interesting afternoons of my travels. Running the bases was fascinating to me. In Finnish baseball, you run to what Americans would call third base, next is first base and then if you make it to the other *third base* you'll get a point. Another point is scored if you make it back to home. And the entire game was played from the pitcher tossing the ball vertically from home plate giving an advantage to the offense.

"Team events are a big hit!"

If I were to try and go into more details on Finnish baseball, I will get them wrong. Even still, I'm probably going to get an email from someone I met commenting on the previous paragraph. But the good news is most people will not be reading this book to learn how to play Finnish baseball.

The fact is I spent an entire afternoon playing the game, and I am still confused on the exact rules. But I'd learned enough to run the bases and know where to catch and throw the ball in the field. I successfully played with the team and made new friendships with people I had just met.

The team event was successful. I had a fun interview with three of the women who had communicated with me the most during our afternoon together. We laughed on and off camera, took a couple of selfies and one kind lady gave me a ride to the bus stop to help navigate me back to the city of Helsinki. In spite of lacking Finnish baseball skills, I'd formed new relationships in a few short hours.

I'm not using a business event to articulate this concept because I believe the point becomes more real in the foreign land of Finland. It's harder to communicate in a foreign country as you fumble through conversations in a language you do not speak. Not only does your sales team speak the same language, they are all doing the same position. Best practices, ideas and efficiencies are often shared amongst sales reps during a team event. You'll want to introduce your new person into this environment to give them access to a more diverse and greater learning culture.

New hires will benefit from a tenured individual mentoring them. But forced communication never prospers as well as a friendship. Instruct your new hire to seek out a friendship with one of the top representatives on your team as it will impact their career to have the personal coaching of a mentor. Encourage one of your top representatives to do the same as it will impact their growth in leadership. By encouraging the right relationship, a mentor will be in place after a well-orchestrated team event.

Trusted Communication

I am in the car with my new friend, Liisa, on our way to venture around the city. As she is fluent in English, I am further provided with a comfortable environment to learn more about the city and culture. Our first stop is the island of Suomenlinna. After a short drive, we are on a boat headed for a sea fortress built on the island.

Liisa lined up our arrival time to coordinate with an English-speaking tour guide. As we are guided around the fortress, I feel thankful for Steve's recommendation to alter my plans and see Finland on my way to Cyprus. The tour has been educational, but my conversation with Liisa has me feeling at home. I enjoy sharing my travel plans, concepts for the book and hearing her insights on leadership.

While this is our first and only day together, I trust Liisa because of her preparation and work to secure enjoyment in my previous day's travel. We are heading back to Helsinki to a popular sauna location where many locals gather year-round to enjoy conversation, drinks and a dip in the Baltic Sea. To round out my entire Finnish experience, I trusted Liisa that I would not have a heart attack from jumping in the cold water after the sauna. And as I am still able to write, I am happy to report I survived.

Continued Communication

From Helsinki, I have taken a short ferry ride to Tallinn, Estonia, as my last stop prior to heading back to Stockholm. It's the seventh day of my trip, and I am making my first attempt at landing an interview with a leader of a foreign country.

I ring the doorbell of the building for the Estonian Reform Party in the capital, Tallinn, and receive an expected, strange look once someone answers the door. But I hand him my marketing material and quickly explain what I am looking to accomplish. My initial contact is extremely nice and welcomes me inside.

I've established my credibility, and the gatekeeper is willing to help. He leaves the room to discuss my situation with the gentleman I will need to talk to for my request. In this situation, the right person agrees to meet me on my initial cold call. Thirty minutes later, I am provided with instructions for next steps. I need to email him and explain in detail what I am looking to accomplish along with the interview questions I will ask. He will then forward this on to the right person to articulate my request for an interview with the former Prime Minister and active VP of the Estonian Parliament, Taavi Rõivas.

I have been informed that Rõivas will not be able to meet while I am here. My short timeline and his schedule aren't going to work. But I am determined to follow-up and schedule the interview at a later date, because I am particularly interested in Estonia's push of technology and education for their youth and country. This is a subject I want to investigate more as I know of Rõivas's involvement in this structured approach to learning and growth.

I'm not sure if my continued communication will lead to an interview. But ceasing communication never produces results. Too often sales managers become comfortable with their top performers, and they no longer offer these elite reps the same communication benefits as their other employees. Your communication with these individuals is as important as conversing with your new hires. When an employee feels unappreciated or lacks continued coaching, production by tenured reps will decrease. This is also a catalyst for a top performer looking to a new company.

I am headed back to Stockholm on another cruise boat after my Helsinki and Tallinn adventures. I am proud of my most unusual route in navigating myself to Cyprus. I, excitedly, write during my time in Stockholm, I am pleased my initial adventures correlate with the leadership concepts for the beginning of this book.

Untrusted Communication

My flight out of Sweden is set up with another unusual flight schedule. My ticket is a flight leaving Stockholm early morning to arrive in Riga, Latvia, before noon. The flight out of Riga to Cyprus isn't until almost midnight. By buying myself a ticket with another large layover; I've added another *Iceland adventure* to my travels for more designed chaos. Or, so I thought.

I have been at the Stockholm airport for the past four hours after arriving at 6:45 a.m. post a one-hour bus ride. When I checked in, I was informed that I was on a much later flight to Riga than originally scheduled. To get back on my original flight, I'd need to call customer service. But I do not believe this will provide me with a solution I want to hear.

The original purchase, when I was planning the trip in San Diego, was an unfortunate experience. Right after I booked the flight, I emailed the customer service department. I was curious if I could bump my twelve-hour layover to the next day for additional time in Latvia. It was an interesting response as I would need to buy one ticket to Riga and another to Larnaca, Cyprus, for my request. This would double the price. They further responded that I'd signed my name as Jonathan as opposed to Jon. Apparently, I'd booked the ticket under Jon, not my full name, Jonathan.

I was appreciative for the response. It appeared signing up for their frequent flyer miles imported my name as Jon and not what I'd typed for the flight. I didn't even catch it. I'd simply logged into the rewards program as I finalized my travel. I happily replied the correct spelling on my passport was Jonathan and thanked them for catching the error.

The next email shocked me. Although this correspondence occurred within twenty-four hours of my purchase with an explanation of what happened, I was told it would cost €50 to change the name on my ticket. I did not have much of an option with the ticket name not matching my passport.

If I hadn't planned this trip on such a tight timeline, I would have rolled the dice on the ticket for Jon Markwardt being good enough for my passport of Jonathan Markwardt. But, I was determined to see Riga and didn't want to buy a whole new ticket at the Stockholm Airport. After two more emails with the customer service department pleading my case, I gave up. It was worth the money to have the original ticket I booked as one I could fly on.

But now, I don't trust the customer service department with my new problem. Halfheartedly, I play along as this later flight is going to cut into the time allotted to explore Riga on my way to Cyprus. I make the international call. Hold music is frustrating when you have nothing else to do. Scrambling to make a flight and knowing each minute is costing me, the ten minutes of hold time feels like an eternity.

After providing my confirmation number and explaining the situation, the lady informs me the earlier flight has been cancelled. This is the closest flight to my original booking. Well, it happens. But I would have loved the additional hours of sleep had I known this was the situation. I woke up at 4:45 a.m. to make this flight.

Apparently, I should have received an email. I pull the phone away from my ear to see the delayed flight message had come while I was on the bus to the airport. She goes on to explain I will still make my connection to Larnaca and there is nothing to worry about.

When I explain what I am trying to do, I am given another option. If I am willing to hop on a sister airline, I can fly to Copenhagen, then Riga. This will get me in an hour and a half earlier to Riga than my current flight.

I pause and calculate the risk and reward of the additional ninety minutes. Not only does the lady on the phone seem credible, but her English is perfect. I enjoy communicating with her and want to trust her. But my current ticket will still allow me to go into Riga for dinner and walk around the city for a few hours. I'd already had one cancelled flight and a debacle of a name-change situation.

Any leader who lies or misleads their people will create an environment of turnover, which will eventually lead to the manager being removed, either by their own accord or the company doing so. An employee needs to have confidence that their leader is watching out for their career. This may mean something different for each individual on the team, so a leader must be adaptable to each employee's aspirations.

In my case, I am uncertain if the person on the phone is truly concerned about my goal of visiting Riga on my way to Cyprus. While I want the additional ninety minutes, the airline has lost my trust. I decline the earlier flight and hope to not be cancelled on, again. Trust is necessary to have positive communication. Without trust, there's no way to show you care if someone doesn't believe you. Care, trust, attitude and communication are intertwined as necessary attributes of a leader. And none of these components matter if you are unprepared to lead your team.

Emotions Affect Communication

When we're faced with bumps in the road, we may not face adversity the best way. We could lose trust through these emotional decisions. Trust can never be regained. Keep your attitude positive (as discussed in Chapter 2). Having a positive outlook will assist you in doing the right thing instead of scrambling for a quick fix.

Your communication will play an important role in the culture and environment of your team. While a sales role can be a sensitive position, it's your job to make sure you are able to help your representatives separate their emotions from the facts. Remember, sales will be fun if we combat rejection with math. All you have to do is keep dialing to get your next opportunity. Leaders keep their communication direct and non-emotional.

Keep this point in mind as you create an environment of trust as a leader through straightforward communication on your team. Your trust will be questioned if your team does not operate on a fair playing field. Everyone needs to follow the same rules. And while rules are, occasionally, meant to be broken, it is important consistency is followed for an honest culture.

A team with an honest culture will do the right thing without the leader's involvement. Foster this environment by providing the members of your team with the opportunity to settle their own disagreements. Plan on discussing policy with each team member and make sure they look at the situation from both sides. It is important to, once again, turn to the facts and not let disputes become emotional. You'll find a trusting and positive environment will provide a culture of communication on the team without your direct involvement.

Before advancing to the next chapter, take a look at your own team communication. You must create an environment of honesty and trust for positive communication to take place. Allow your new hire to see these interactions as you onboard them to the team. In your new hire's first week, add the following three items to expand their communication within your company.

1. Book ride-a-long time with your best sales reps.

2. Add a team event to the employee's calendar.

3. Schedule time with other departments, including but not limited to operations, to shadow as part of the onboarding process.

5

Autopsy–No Air Conditioning

Despite the hiccups and exhausting travel, I keep my attitude positive to enjoy my stopover in Riga. I make a friend, Nicola, on the bus into the city, and we decide to explore the city together. He is a young man traveling from Spain for a three-day project on leadership for young professionals from multiple countries.

Nicola has my attention as I question him about leadership. "What type of leader would you want to follow?" He gives a simple response. "A good leader is someone you would like to become."

While not directly stating it, his answer indicates a leader needs to provide learning and growth. To become someone means growing one's own knowledge and experience to a higher level. In one sentence, he communicates his understanding of a leader.

We are eating dinner together at a traditional Latvian restaurant, but I get up quickly to exit. Through all our conversations on leadership, I lost track of time and need to scramble back to the airport. I make my late evening flight and settle in for some rest as the plane quietly sails across the night sky.

Leaders are Efficient

I land in Cyprus at nearly 4 a.m., and am back to where I wrote my first book. The buses don't start running for another two hours to get me to where I am staying in Protaras, but I am excited to be home on the island.

Looking at my calendar, I'm wondering if I have allotted enough time for the number of places I want to go and the people I want to see; I am fortunate to have made life-long friends on the island. While I will be in Cyprus for fifteen days, I know they will go by quickly. I need to be efficient with my time while I am here in order to stay on schedule. The importance of my next destination, Poland, and the search for my family roots is a priority that will keep me moving.

My first week on the island goes by in a flash. The enjoyment of visiting beautiful beaches and spending time with friends seem to shorten the hours in a day. With a busy schedule and late nights, I don't enjoy early mornings. But when there is an opportunity worthwhile, I jump out of bed. And today is such a day. My friend and illustrator from my first and now second book, Penelope Constantinou, wants to meet in the capital. Our plan is to visit and discuss illustrations for the book. She further agrees to provide me with direction on my struggle to get an interview with the President of Cyprus.

Despite multiple emails over the two months leading up to my travels with no response, I find myself believing things will work out. Either way, I am looking forward to visiting with my friend in Nicosia. It has been two years since we've seen each other, and it will be fun to catch up. Although she isn't sure how to help with the interview other than showing me where to go for an in-person attempt, I am appreciative. Confidence is gained when we have people cheering us on.

Cyprus has a special meaning to my family, so I want to, once again, write it into my travels in a unique way. I wrote my first book on the island as a tribute to my uncle, Gary Markwardt, who lived in Nicosia for three years. In 1998, Gary passed away from a glioblastoma. This rare form of cancer has appeared twice in my life and has given me the courage to follow my dreams with the reminder that life is short.

It seemed fitting to include the memory of my uncle as I was on a search for our family history. Not only was he a good man, but he is still inspiring me and others to follow their dreams. His legacy provides inspiration through my aunt, Lissa Markwardt, who is a life coach and continually shares his story to encourage the masses to live their life now.

Leaders are Prepared for Anything

It's 6 a.m., and I am on the bus working on my computer as everyone seated around me sleeps. I've done my research on the President and am well abreast on current events and the political issues of the country. I do not plan on going in-depth or necessarily discussing any of these topics. But I always commit myself to a process of preparation. And this situation is no different.

Upon arriving, I am able to touch base with Penelope and find out she will not be able to meet until the afternoon. Since I am going on a true cold call, I decide to make the venture to the Presidential Palace on my own. I am no stranger to the art of cold calling. So, I hop in a taxi with a destination that surprises the driver.

We arrive at a large gate and a long driveway. The taxi driver takes me through the entry, but has to stop earlier than I would have expected. He instructs me to get out. I start my cold call standing in front of a guard station with barbed wire, a gate and two men in uniform. I have just changed into my long-sleeved dress shirt, and I am holding my sports jacket on a hanger. In mere seconds, I start sweating in the summer heat. At this moment, I don't feel like there is anything cold about this call. But worse, the two gentlemen in uniform are looking at me like I am an alien from another planet.

Leaders Prepare Marketing Material

I quickly start to explain myself as I realize the awkwardness of the situation. While this isn't what I'd envisioned, I am still prepared. I hand one of the gentleman my large speaker card as I introduce myself.

"My name is Jon Markwardt, and I'm an American author from San Diego, California, writing a book on leadership. I'm looking for ten minutes with President Anastasiades to highlight him in my book."

I've found no matter what the situation, educational marketing material can quickly establish credibility. As the guard flips the 8.5" x 11" speaker card over front to back multiple times, it appears he is looking at a foreign object he's never seen before. While your team may never be in a similar situation to this, please reflect on your own marketing material. Are you prepared for your collateral to educate prospects and increase credibility for the members on your team?

By sheer body language, I can tell the gentleman has transferred his apprehensive feelings to curiosity. I continue to explain my story—my deceased uncle having lived in Nicosia, the other interviews I am doing, and the first book being written in Cyprus with a Cypriot doing the illustrations. I name-drop a couple of the contacts who have been attempting to help me obtain an interview, and now, the questioning of why I am here has turned to his predicament of not knowing how he can assist me.

The guard sounds frustrated as he repeats what I'd now heard multiple times. "I am only allowed to let people in with an appointment."

My wheels are turning. "I can only remember one of my contacts inside the Presidential Palace." Upon mentioning the name, it comes with great relief when he knows the person. Even if it isn't the right person, he has now warmed up to me from his initial shock of my arrival.

He makes a few phone calls. And since my Greek is comparable to my Finnish, I can't begin to understand what is being discussed. But the body language and tone seem positive; however, the result is not as he only agrees to pass my information to the person he determined should take it. Thankfully, he allows me to write down this new contact's phone number and email address.

Sometimes, you make a sales call to get another sales call. However, in this instance, not only am I not getting an appointment today, I am not getting a meeting at any point in the foreseeable future. I am left standing at the front gate sweating profusely with my taxi driver long gone in the distance.

Due to appropriate planning in-case of being granted an interview, my backpack is full of cameras, tripods, microphones and two lights. Not only is it heavy, but it is providing great warmth to my back. I set the backpack on the ground as sweat drips down my forehead.

I will not be getting into the building today. And worse, the guard motions his finger to the end of the long driveway as the direction I need to go. "Your taxi driver is gone." This guard is not providing me with new information. I am not blind. I know the taxi left; I paid him and told him to leave.

No part of me even considered having my taxi driver wait because leaders prepare for an optimal outcome. And while my positive attitude is the right decision, I am now stranded with no taxi or even a helpful destination at the end of the driveway.

6th Attribute: Urgency

I convince the guards to call a taxi to pick me up. It is my only sale of the day—thus far. But it is a crucial one—I was going to strip down to my boxers if I was forced to make this walk with my heavy backpack. I know this would be inappropriate and would secure that I never get an interview. But at 95 degrees and sweating profusely, I am thinking about air conditioning equal to my body's need for oxygen and water.

It's a common belief that our most basic needs must be taken care of before we can strive for anything greater. In my situation, I'm unable to strategically plan for a future interview unless my need for air conditioning is met.

When an employee's basic needs are not met, there will be no way for you to keep the employee around for the long-term. The quick lesson on how this applies to leadership is if you are underpaying your employees, not providing them with minimal benefits, requiring overtime hours or providing poor working conditions; you will have turnover no matter how great of a leader you may be. An employee will only grow within a company when all of their basic needs are met. Leaders recognize employee needs and strategically address them in advance to avoid turnover from inadequate prioritization of their sales representatives.

My intense need for air conditioning illustrates our sixth attribute required of leaders: urgency. An elite leader will have a high sense of urgency to provide their employees with what is needed most. While managers may delay necessary activities, leaders will take initiative to build the success of their team as quickly as possible. There is no job description needed for a leader, because their job is to build an elite team and will tackle all tasks to do so.

While a manager needs to be told their responsibilities, a leader consistently takes on greater activity to contribute to their team's success. If you do everything you are asked, you are fantastic in your position. But that's it. Initiative is the primary way to push learning and growth as a leader. The urgency to take on these greater tasks will drive new results that your own manager has never seen.

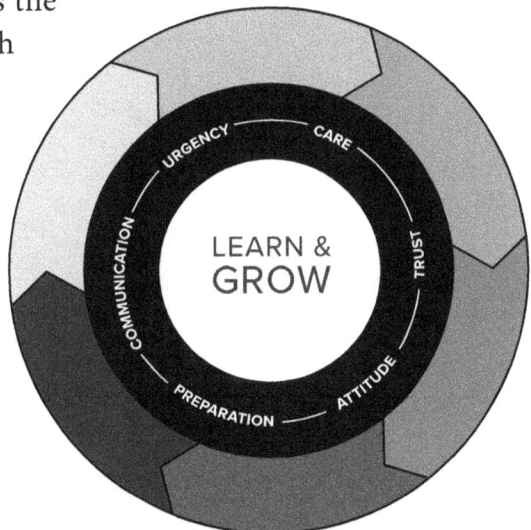

Markwardt's Wheel of Leadership

The Leadership Wheel provides a template of attributes necessary for elite leaders, requirements for the company and an outline of how to build and grow an elite team in your current position. This formula for success should be passed on to your sales reps to grow leaders on your team. There is no portion of the Leadership Wheel greater than any other in order to complete the Wheel. All are required for a leader to perform at an elite level.

Each leader must operate as a wheel in continuous motion. While a perfect wheel would be built segment-by-segment, life and leadership do not work this way. Leaders must concentrate on the entire Leadership Wheel at all times to achieve elite success. This overview of the entire Wheel

"Little wins are necessary for bigger wins."

is crucial to grasp the challenge at hand in growing leaders. While our first five chapters detailed necessary leadership attributes, the remainder of the book will outline how to systematically build a perennial, elite team by accomplishing the requirements of elite leadership.

Attributes of Leadership

The center of our Leadership Wheel emphasizes the greatest need of a leader as their ability to create an environment where employees can learn and grow. This is the foundation of the Wheel and of every elite leader. Our first five chapters established the leadership characteristics necessary for learning and growth to take place. These six attributes collectively form the inner circle around the center of the Wheel. Each attribute contributes to fostering a culture of learning and growth.

1st Attribute: Care

This means you should not be in a leadership position if you do not care about your people. Specifically, a leader must care about helping their sales reps learn and grow in their careers. A leader is not necessarily your best friend but helps push you to greater heights because they care to do so.

2nd Attribute: Trust

It is impossible to learn in an environment where there isn't trust. If someone is continually questioning their leader, they will not follow this person for long. Carr's illustration of intellectual honesty taught us how this attribute has affected his entire career.

3rd Attribute: Attitude

The leader must have a positive attitude as this allows the leader to minimize the bumps in the road. This is required to continue their employees on a path of learning and growth for the betterment of their career. No one can achieve elite success in a negative environment.

4th Attribute: Preparation

Each leader must be prepared to grow an employee's career. This requires a leader to be in a constant state of learning. If they are not ready to teach their employees, there will not be a plan of education. Without an outline of instruction, the leader will rely on hope. And this is not a strategy for learning and growth.

5th Attribute: Communication

The most vital attribute for the Wheel's center piece will be communication. If the employee does not communicate what they do not understand, proper learning cannot take place. Two-way communication on a regular basis will be required to grow your relationship with your employee and their career.

6th Attribute: Urgency

Finally, no leader can achieve success without proper urgency to the task at hand. An elite leader knows when to shift focus for their team. Leadership cannot thrive passively, but flourishes through initiative for the strategic growth of the team. Elite leaders will urgently water their grass wherever necessary to cover every inch of their yard with the greenest grass on the block.

Requirements of Leadership

The attributes form the inner circle of the Leadership Wheel, which all contribute to an elite team's core need of learning and growth. The outer circle comprises the six requirements of an elite leader. It is impossible to take care of your employee's needs when the leader's needs are not taken care of. A dehydrated person will love a glass of water more than their significant other. So, it's important for a leader's needs to be met in order to concentrate on their employees and growing the greater good of the company. If you can't lead yourself, you will not be able to lead anyone else.

Requirement 1: Benefits Package

Leadership is dependent on building a team for the long haul. There can't be any short-cuts or quick fixes. As a leader, your time commitment is necessary to grow the right culture and build the team with a greater purpose. This requires the basic needs of a leader to be met so they aren't looking elsewhere. These minimal requirements to their employment package include above average pay, benefits and a belief in the product or service along with the company.

Notice, the stipulation is above average pay. In most cases, this will need to be achieved by hitting sales goals. Your on-target earnings (OTE) will determine if the pay meets this objective. This means what you will be paid when you are hitting a fair quota as a manager.

It should be above average as long as you are performing. If you believe you are fairly paid, underpaid or fighting an unrealistic quota; you will be open to receive recruiter calls. This entertainment of other opportunities will include the possibility of going back into sales and abandoning leadership all together. No one can be a leader without a commitment to the growth of the individuals and team for the long-term, so each leader requires a healthy employee benefits package.

Requirement 2: Job Security

All leaders operate differently under pressure. There is a time and place to be scrutinized for not hitting a quota. And this should occur for a leader when it becomes a pattern. You should welcome the scrutiny if you have a fair quota and are failing to hit your number. But for an elite leader to take form, job security from a company perspective and your own career must be achieved.

A leader questioning whether the company wants them around cannot build for the long haul. They must shift and manage to their immediate goals for the survival of their current position. Similar to the belief in their own future, the leader must believe the company will be around for the long-term and continue to grow. If they believe the company will downsize or ultimately dissolve, the leader's job security will be compromised for themselves and their team.

Requirement 3: Network

There is a fine line in the sand with direct reports. A leader may struggle if too great of social bonds are made with their employees. Therefore, the network of a leader cannot be built solely with their team. At the same time, every leader needs to have rapport with each team member as the most basic form of networking.

Leaders need to have a constant pulse of what's going on within the company, because leadership is best not served on an island. This is achieved through connections outside of your team. This higher level of networking builds relationships with the executives of the company, peers, recruiters, administrative individuals and operational staff. This requirement is achieved as close friendships blossom from this internal network in your company.

Requirement 4: Recognition

Managers can often become more concerned with their own recognition over the individuals on their team. Leaders do not publicly speak of their own income, stress or rewards. Your recognition as a leader does not stem from your own devices. It is built on the individual's goals, success and achievements of those on your team.

The greatest recognition a leader will ever feel is the fulfillment from positively influencing the career and life of an individual. Your need for recognition as a leader will be met as sales reps on your team make more money, achieve new heights in their career and individually thank you for the contributions you've made. Consequently, this will occur as the team grows and gains recognition on its own. Your income and personal recognition increases in coordination with the representatives on your team. Concentrate on your sales reps and your recognition needs will be met as a leader.

Requirement 5: Elite Success

Elite success is a quantitative measurement required to be an elite leader. And it is achieved upon building a successful team and striving to provide each member of the team with the greatest opportunity in their current role. This is the level in which your team has achieved success and you remove obstacles other teams will continue to deal with as the team strives for an elite status recognized by the company through rank and percentage of quota.

Additional opportunities are provided by the leader in this stage. This may mean individual sales at a minimal level, and on the upmost level it would mean a new franchise relationship, partnership or national account created by the leader and filtered to the team members individually. These favorable circumstances are not available on other teams as they are generated by the team's leader in coordination with the efforts of each individual on the team.

This phase takes the team to being the best they can possibly be. It creates an environment of winning, fun and a culture no one wants to break away from. Ironically, this stage often results in assisting sales reps to advance from your team as they grow their own careers into leadership or other desired positions.

Requirement 6: Greater Good

For an elite leader to truly be formed, there must be something bigger accomplished than forming an elite sales team. This requirement is a stage of implementation for new opportunities through programs, processes and expanded relationships for the greater good of the company. This can only be achieved at the highest level through the sales representative's propelling this stage forward. It cannot be accomplished by one individual, but is achieved collectively by the entire team.

The greatest test of leadership is how the individuals on the team conduct themselves when the leader is not around. A greater good is more likely to be attained when the leader and individuals are chasing a goal for the company that has fulfillment associated with it. This cause will be chased at full speed whether the leader is present or not. This is the result of everyone on the team taking ownership of the greater good. Ultimately, this pursuit becomes infectious for other teams and the company as a new culture is born and career opportunities are advanced for all in the sales organization.

Wheels Move

Prior to moving on to the next chapter, please re-read the above components of the Leadership Wheel. It is important to have a good overview of the Wheel before we discuss each segment in detail with what is necessary for each leadership stage. Write in the space below the requirements you need to strengthen and write three action items you can work on for growth in these areas.

As you read the remaining chapters, your top three action items will change. Write these in pencil and be open to whatever it takes to build each segment on the Wheel. As a leader, your role and Wheel will constantly be moving. You must be able to work on your Requirement 4 needs as you push towards a higher level in Requirement 1. Update your action items as you continue to grow your leadership career to a complete and functioning Wheel. Do not use any of the requirements as an excuse for failure but a guidebook to build your elite success.

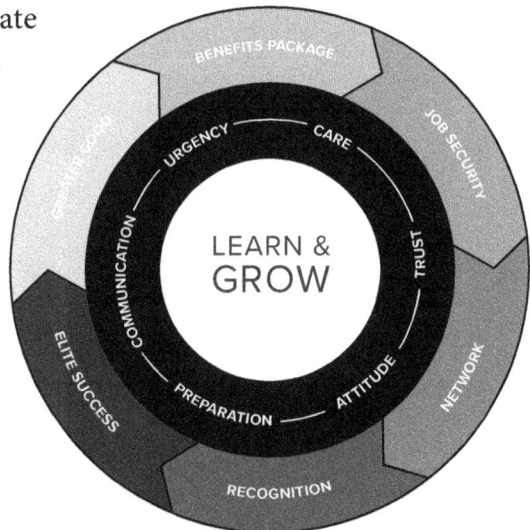

Hence, your action items should be things you can control. It should not be a wish list given to upper management.

Leadership Requirements:

_____

_____

_____

_____

_____

Action items for growth:

1. _____

_____

2. _____

_____

3. _____

_____

6

Scooter Suit

Our first five chapters established the core attributes required of leaders. These qualities are necessary components to assist in building each requirement of the Leadership Wheel. It will take effort to build the core of your own Wheel as characteristics of leaders develop over time.

Failure becomes necessary in the path to success for each leader as they develop their careers. But one failure is an opportunity for a different success. And with high activity, success can be predicted and expected.

My own failure from the sweaty visit to the barbed wire fence had me discouraged. But I kept my attitude positive as I followed up with the contact I was given from the guard. While there ended up being a great deal of correspondence to coordinate an interview, I never made it past the gate.

Failure Breeds Success

My failure in Estonia inevitably had a better outcome than my quest to interview the active President of Cyprus. I had been emailing back and forth since the day of my initial cold call to secure an interview date and time to sit down with Rõivas. Coincidently, it was the day after my barbed wire fiasco when I received a confirmation email for the date and time of the interview to take place in the Estonian Parliament Building.

I now have to make my way back to Tallinn on my travels. While I am anxious to get to Poland and search for my family history, my travel plans must be altered as the interview will take priority for the importance of this book. As discussed, leadership must operate as a wheel and constantly be moving to the greatest need. Thus, my itinerary changed overnight.

My cold calls are a unique way to go about getting an interview with a world leader. These attempts illustrate failure, and articulate that we all have endless opportunities disregarding immediate connections. Success is secured by taking an urgent approach to persistence, dedication and hard work. We all have the capability of achieving these attributes. The elite pursue them longer and harder than everyone else due to their urgency to take care of their team's needs.

I believe a lot can be accomplished with a cold call. If someone will talk to me in person, I have a far better chance of gaining a desired result over following any type of formal phone call or email process others will often choose. Please keep in mind most of my failing stories did not make the book, so this story of success resulted from numerous failures. But the positivity I give cold calling should be noted as most sales individuals and leaders do not enjoy the task. What message does your attitude send to your team about cold calling?

I tend to exaggerate my own needs—as air conditioning became a requirement for life in the last chapter. My urgency has me fighting for higher level items like someone else would battle for their own survival with food, water or oxygen. While it seems extreme, leaders operate with a determination others do not. This urgency creates action and results for the team as this drive is set from the top down. What message are you sending to the members of your team by your urgency to work past failure and achieve results?

Urgency Creates Results

I'll happily explain my urgent needs on a random Thursday. I need a haircut and a new suit as much as I need food and water. As a result of Rõivas having other important meetings after our scheduled interview, he would be unable to dress casual for the meeting.

It is typical for me to request the interview to be casual as I think how we dress has an effect on how we feel and how we act. In my opinion, the relaxed dress will often get me a more authentic interview. People tend to get more real with their answers when they are dressed casually.

Obviously, I am not deterred when this cannot occur. My day in Cyprus is simply being adjusted for my greatest needs. I feel it will be most appropriate for me to mirror his dress as we will be meeting at the Parliament House. I don't want to be back behind barbed wire if I show up in a t-shirt.

I am on an unusual excursion for a summer day on the island. There are zero tourists coming to the beach to go suit shopping. Well, unless it's a swimsuit they're looking for. I am unsure of where I can find a place to buy a formal suit, so I get a referral from my friend, Pascal. Thankfully, I am able to navigate to the store. I find a new suit, get it tailored and somehow figure out how to transfer it back to my house on a scooter.

I am now a haircut away from accomplishing my urgent needs of the day. And the second place I try has someone speaking perfect English. This is a requirement for me to get a haircut. My Greek is so poor, I would end up with a shaved head if I couldn't find someone who spoke English to cut my hair.

Accomplishing these tasks feels like conquering enormous feats. They put me in a position where I simply need to make

"Urgency drives in a business suit
at 100 degrees."

my travels back to Estonia. I am prepared for the interview and I am looking forward to formally adding Rõivas to the book.

Requirement 1: Benefits Package

While the objective of turning greater tasks to a high level of urgency is important, it does not summarize our first requirement needs of the Leadership Wheel. As the overview stated in the last chapter, your own benefits package must be met as it is impossible to adequately care for someone else without your basic needs taken care of. Leadership requires a commitment to the long haul of building your team and doing so because you care about each member of your team individually.

It is important you commit to growing the greenest grass on the block while also acknowledging that your timeline to success may take time. If your potential earnings, benefits or belief in the product, service or company are not up to par; it would be better to take a *Grass Is Greener* approach on your situation. You must put yourself in a yard you are committed to watering to complete the entire Wheel.

If you didn't just close the book to look for another leadership position, it is important for you to be thankful and embrace the situation you are in. You have great income potential and benefits; you believe in your company. It is

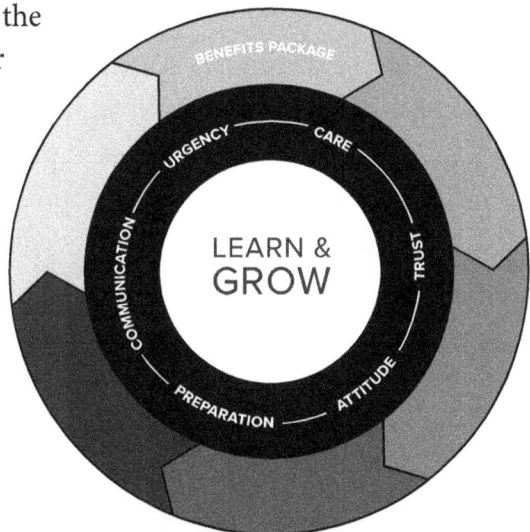

important you recognize your own employee benefits package. You are in a respectable position to provide for yourself and family. There are people not as fortunate as you.

Some people take a job solely to have income. You have a career opportunity. It is important that you take the good from your opportunity as a reason to believe *The Grass is Browner on the Other Side*. You are in a fortunate situation, and you have the opportunity to fully commit to watering your lawn. And this is necessary for the greater good of your team and career. All of your lower level needs are being met with your employee benefits.

Higher Level Benefits

If your basic needs are met, you have what is necessary to build your Leadership Wheel. But for complete construction, there are additional priorities in your benefits package. You will have some control over these greater needs with direct communication and interaction with your company. And for those you can't control, you will need to build success through other portions of the Wheel to later strengthen your Requirement 1 needs.

The next important employee benefit as a leader is your ability to have a fully staffed team. There are different ways to take care of this need. But it is important you are able to secure this need or your timeline to build other requirements of the Leadership Wheel will be extended substantially.

You cannot sell someone on love, where to live or their career. Please take a moment and think about each one of those situations. There is a large time investment for each of these examples and there is inherent emotion to these decisions. If someone makes one of these choices they, ultimately, did not want to make, they will navigate from their current disposition or have an attitude of regret. Both results will not allow them to prosper at their current state.

As a basic requirement to your staffing needs, you will need to supply a fair compensation plan aligned with fair benefits for the position. If you don't have this, you will effectively find yourself selling people to come on board. Notice, I am no longer saying above average compensation with benefits. While this would be extremely helpful to your hiring efforts, the leader's need for their employees is they must be fair.

If you have below average pay and benefits, it will require perfect working conditions. You will not be able to work your staff greater than an eight-hour day. They will need standard breaks and random perks such as company lunches and fun activities. Most important, they must be appreciated and recognized by the leader and executives of the company.

I detail all of this for those leading in strained conditions. Treating your employees properly and with respect still applies for those managing well paid individuals with benefits. But lower income with less credible benefits require the environment to be flawless. Even with a perfect environment, you will have turnover as your team looks to increase their own needs elsewhere. But without creating a respectful culture, your turnover will be at a rate exponentially higher than you will be able to overcome through any amount of hiring efforts.

Basic benefits must be met in life and business. Should turnover occur in poor conditions, know this is an expected result. You should manage according to the current state. You will need to work towards changing the structure of how your individuals are paid, or look for a position where this obstacle does not deter you from building your Leadership Wheel.

Recruiting

It will be crucial for a recruiter or multiple recruiters to be in place based on the staffing needs and employee benefits for the sales representatives. If you have been given a fully staffed team with above average pay and benefits, the amount of time you'll need to allocate to recruiting efforts should cover the needs for staffing your team. Outside of this situation, you will require the support of a recruiter.

Please note if you do not have a recruiter and your position is to scale and staff your team, you are not in a leadership position. You are a recruiter. You will be able to recruit on your own and grow your team to a level where you have the opportunity to be a leader. But do not confuse yourself on what your position is.

There is nothing wrong with being a recruiter, but leaders must lead themselves before they lead others. And as a recruiter, you need to lead yourself to a fully staffed team. Some leaders do not make good recruiters. And other leaders are the best recruiters I've ever seen. Whatever situation you fall into, it is crucial your urgency to hire become that of a recruiter if this is your role and responsibility. Respectively, you will not be able to complete the first requirement of the Leadership Wheel as you are not in a leadership position, yet.

It is crucial you recruit with the same sense of urgency I had for my new suit and haircut. The following chapters will not only help you recruit but will also allow you to understand the Leadership Wheel you are building once you are fully staffed. I am not a recruiter. Two times in my career, I found myself in a recruiting position. My overall capacity to be the leader I am capable of being was compromised in both situations.

I understood my own employee needs along with my desires and capabilities. Subsequently, I advanced my career from both of these positions in direct relation to my needs not being met. No one acts at their peak capacity when they are struggling for basic requirements. It is important you secure a recruiting solution to staff your team without this becoming your full-time role. And if you choose to make it your responsibility, you must scramble with a high sense of urgency to make it your part time position once you scale the team through your own efforts.

Employee Benefit Expectations

A leader's employee benefit package as described in this chapter is necessary to grow their career for the long term. For our Leadership Wheel, these needs include more than pay, health insurance and a 401k. As discussed earlier, expectations should be set from the first interview by a leader. This becomes a need for the leader as well because without an environment of open and honest communication, you will not be able to continue to build your Wheel. A leader must be able to trust the expectations set by the company.

Expectations mean consistency. This is a consistency to a compensation plan, sales policies, minimum activity levels, working hours and conduct within the office, team and company. Should your expectations provide inconsistency to you or your team, this will create opportunities for turnover. There should not be a mass exodus from an adjustment, but the greater the change or lack of consistency creates an environment of turnover due to lack of trust.

This is often outside of the leader's control. I know leaders who deal with a compensation plan change every year. I know numerous start-ups consistently change polices, expectations and metrics. As we learned from Bob Carr, this is where the leader must exercise intellectual honesty. At the foremost of expectations, your team must be able to expect honesty from their leader to formulate a culture of trust.

Cohesive Work Environment

The open and honest culture is the true need for the leader. Most companies will have expectations change. Your consistency on being able to articulate the changes directly with your team will be crucial for your credibility as a leader and handling this most basic need.

Furthermore, there must be a consistency across the company. In kind, you will need a company culture supporting honest and direct communication. If you instruct your team one way, it will be impossible for you to maintain credibility if other teams do not follow suit.

The best way to articulate this would be a sales policy adversely affecting the members of your team. If your team follows this new direction acting with intellectual honesty, it is crucial the other teams play fair. If they do not, an environment has been created where it becomes financially better for an individual working for a leader without intellectual honesty.

While your ethics are not being challenged, your credibility for providing your team with an equal playing field will be. Unless you are an executive of the company, it will be hard to overcome this type of environment. We'll discuss later how Requirement 3 of our Wheel can effect greater change for you, your team and the company should these types of situations arise. This once again illustrates how you must be working on the entire Wheel as opposed to one requirement at a time.

This brings us to a cohesive work environment as our last need of the leader's benefit package. No matter how great your leadership skills, you will not establish trust with your team if your individuals are operating in a manner the rest of the company is not adhering to. Minimum activity, rules, policies and company expectations must be universal. If each team and office is creating their own culture, leaders will be questioned as employees compare circumstances and conditions.

As companies move past their large growth phase into the maturity phase, maintaining revenue growth and expectations to the stockholders or investors often becomes a struggle. Without the introduction of new products, services or lines of business, it is often not possible to continue at the same accelerated rate of growth. This is typically where the deterioration of company cohesion occurs. The results become celebrated over the process. And the culture becomes an environment of results first over fair working conditions.

It's time for you to evaluate this chapter and determine if your current benefits package provides you with the ability to operate as a leader, manager or recruiter. Managers and recruiters will work without all aspects of the Requirement 1 needs for elite leadership. They will scramble to hit quotas, metrics and survive in their current situation. A few will have well-recognized careers, enjoy what they do and find fulfillment from the diamonds in the rough they are able to hire, coach and advance in their careers.

There is nothing wrong with managing and recruiting to foster results and achieve success. However, this book was written for those looking to build their careers as leaders. Leadership has everything to do with leading people along a path of growth and learning, and the advancement of the greater good of the company. Managers and recruiters will struggle with the time capacity to concentrate on these items.

Write the employee benefits you are missing as discussed in this chapter for your current role. Once you understand what you need to advance your benefit package, it is your job as a leader to create the impact within your company for these improvements for yourself and peers. Leaders are able to use the higher-level requirements of the Leadership Wheel to push progress in advancing their Requirement 1 needs. Keep reading if you fall into this category and formulate a plan for growth once you have an understanding of the entire Wheel and achieve the recognition necessary to effect change.

_____

_____

_____

_____

_____

_____

7

Triple-A Team

My time in Cyprus is coming to a close. And I have continually failed at an unusual challenge. A good friend of mine, Crina, has never gone snorkeling before. She is scared to put her face underwater and wants nothing to do with it. I have purchased one of the snorkel masks that covers a person's entire face, and I am determined for her to experience the sensation of breathing and looking underwater at the same time.

Unfortunately, my efforts thus far have not even resulted in her trying on the mask. It has been a strong no until today. Crina has traveled with me to Cyprus's own famous Blue Lagoon. This is a much different Blue Lagoon than the one I'd been to in Iceland. It is not a hot spring, but a portion of the Mediterranean Sea where it collides the most vibrant blue colors to create an area of visual stimulation.

I convinced Crina to try the mask on while she is standing waist deep in water, then to lower her head down to the surface. To say it isn't going well is an understatement. Not only can she barely allow her face to look down in the water, but her less-than-one-second view has resulted in her abruptly ripping off the mask and getting out of the sea.

Pressure

I think most people would have given up on helping Crina achieve this goal. But there are times where additional pressure is needed to achieve a desired result. I know she will be safe and enjoy the experience, but she is requiring an additional push.

People often respond to the environment they are in. You may find a shy person able to yell and scream at a sporting event or an outgoing person become nervous when they are on stage. Throughout my life and career, I have observed people will often change their behavior when they are on camera.

Intrinsically, our minds know that if we are being filmed there will be people watching the video, including ourselves. No one wants to watch themselves on video looking scared or embarrassed. Correspondingly, two responses will typically occur if someone is surprised by a video camera.

The first is the person shuts down the experiment and wants nothing to do with you or your camera. They will cover their face and tell you to shut it off. The second is a response of greater courage and awareness to what they are doing. They do not want anyone to see themselves on video afraid or doing something they will later be embarrassed to watch.

Crina has failed three times at snorkeling, so I decide to provide pressure to the situation. She has no idea what she's walked into. But as we stand waist-deep in the Blue Lagoon, I hit record on my GoPro.

"Crina, you're going to snorkel for your first time." I announce. I then explain her fear to the camera and encourage her to overcome it. I can tell she's blind-sided by the look of disgust on her face.

I hand her the mask and tell her to put it on. The mask goes on, and she begins swimming underwater for the first time. I congratulate her and turn the camera off so she can make her own decision to continue. Since she's seen success with the task, she decides to try it again without the camera. She finds the need of coming up to the surface has subsided as she stays underwater longer than her first attempt.

Crina and I snorkel all the way back to the boat, which is about eight hundred meters away. Part of her fear had come from her lack of swimming skills. But swimming face down with ample air makes the task of swimming easier.

Crina began questioning herself on why she'd never tried snorkeling before. Sometimes pressure is needed. Leaders know how and when to apply it in a safe environment to produce a heightened result. Not only do individual sales professionals need this type of encouragement, but it can often times become important for a leader to receive a push for the desired results on their team.

Requirement 2: Job Security

The second requirement of our Leadership Wheel is the need for job security. Our snorkeling experience illustrates the point of pressure being positive and necessary in certain situations. However, we must discuss the fact that tension cannot be applied on a continuous basis. If I find a new way to metaphorically dunk Crina's head underwater every day, she will eventually fail at the task and get frustrated; then our friendship would cease to exist.

This concept will be the same for your sales professionals as it is for leaders. Once again, leadership operates and focuses on the long-term. Management focuses on the immediate results. While, metaphorically, dunking someone's head underwater every day on your sales team may produce results, it will not create the long-term growth and expansion of your team into an elite anomaly. It will create turnover, and the culture you've created will promote this as a company norm to your new hires.

Leaders need to have trust and security in their position for the long term. If this is present for the leader, it will be

"Continual pressure will drown your employees."

available for everyone performing on the team. This means the company must not only be stable, but it must also be growing for your own career and the advancement of the individuals on your team. As a leader, you will, once again, recognize this as an amazing opportunity to grow your green grass exactly where you are at.

Leaders Know Their Numbers

It is important for the job security of you and your team to continuously promote and share company insights. As the leader, you need to know where the company is going and the statistical growth that has occurred. This will create excitement for your team and your potential new hires. This information needs to be shared in interviews and continuously updated during team meetings and one-on-ones. Individuals love hearing they've chosen the right place to be, and that's when the *Grass Is Browner* Culture takes form.

Leaders know company and team statistics. It is extremely important for you to be knowledgeable of your company's employee size, total customers, revenue per unit, total revenue and the company's year-over-year growth. Obviously, the numbers can be endless. You can analyze a business's data

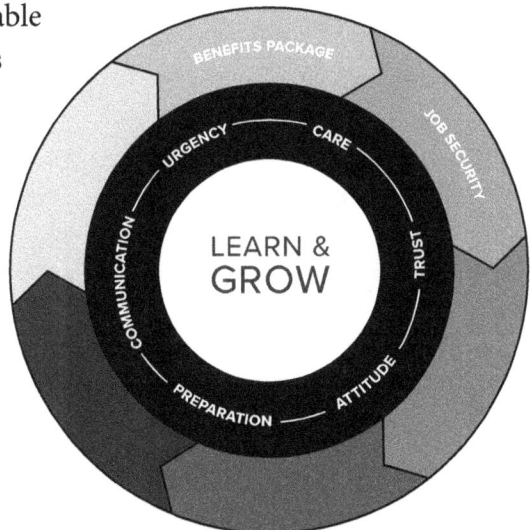

in numerous ways. Appropriately, statistics can be manipulated to the positive. The numbers to share with clients and your direct employees are the stats accentuating the company's growth and positive attributes.

You should know your company's statistics inside and out. And you should be updating these numbers on a quarterly basis for yourself and team. You should have marketing material detailing these statistics and template emails for your team to bullet point the facts of why others should be working with your representatives and company.

Please answer the following questions and respond accordingly to determine your own green grass statistics for your company.

1. Have your statistics been updated in the last 90 days?

2. Does your team have marketing collateral with this data?

3. Is there an email template detailing the company facts of why prospects should be working with your representatives?

4. Do your reps know these numbers?

Marketing Manager

For each one of these questions, you are the sales leader and need to take ownership of the answers. If the marketing team has not created what you need, your action item may include requesting material from your marketing department. It is important these materials are constantly updated to provide a new look, accurate statistics and excitement for your prospects and employees.

If the marketing department does not have adequate documents available, create them for your team. You must make sure your information proudly displays your company. You may need to reach out to numerous departments to secure proper data and gain help to proudly display this information on a one-page marketing slick. You are the leader, and these materials contribute job security within the company for you and your team. Consequently, you are the marketing manager as well if there isn't a department to assist you.

As a leader, each document and template you provide will be seen in abundance by prospects. Are you helping your sales professionals increase their closing ratio with the marketing collateral? If not, invest in resources to assist you.

The task of creating marketing material articulates an action item for leaders striving for an elite team. These leaders take their own initiative with the same urgency I had for air conditioning, a haircut and a new business suit. They are not prompted by who they report to or from a request by someone on their team. Essential pieces to build your team for the long-term fall on your plate whether someone articulates this to you or not.

By choosing to tackle these tasks on your own, it allows your sales team to concentrate on selling. These contributions to their daily routine will increase closing ratios for gaining new appointments and sales. Embrace new responsibilities as a leader so you can continue to build your Leadership Wheel. Not only does this help grow your team, but it furthers your job security as this initiative is seen and recognized by upper management.

You Can't Lose

As discussed earlier, there are times when pressure needs to be applied. An employee will only feel the awkwardness of the situation if their leader does not supply direct communication. If you are forthright, it is simply business, and it is appropriate everyone receive accurate and timely feedback.

When you are in a situation requiring your representative to feel the strain, it is imperative your communication be direct and honest. You will cite specific examples of where the representative has failed in their performance, outline their statistics and provide them with a timeline to correct their behavior. Be blunt in communicating that their employment may not continue if they do not immediately correct their performance issues.

It is important to say, "may not continue". The "may" gives you an option if the representative has progressed in an appropriate manner to extend the timeline for the employee to get their numbers where they need to be. Your company policies and insight into the individual will determine how to proceed.

If they do not turn their behavior around in your required timeline, it is better for your security as a leader to terminate the employee and move on. Ultimately, a failing employee is a failing employee. *There are, of course, exceptions to this rule.* But as long as you have been candid with the employee, the individual will know this result is coming. It becomes a simple business transaction as to why you will not continue working together.

You cannot lose if you are direct with a failing employee. They will either succeed or your underperforming employee will no longer be a distraction for your team as you hire someone else. One of these two results must occur to provide you with a situation where you will win.

You must be prepared for an employee's termination so you never lose. You should constantly be interviewing for top sales performers. But your urgency for hiring will increase when an employee is on a termination timeline due to performance.

Unfortunately, companies fall victim to not following through with eliminating failing employees. This can result from various fears. A company could be so far behind in their staffing efforts that terminating a bad employee becomes a perceived, poor solution to upper management or investors. I write "perceived" on purpose as it is always the right decision to get rid of underperforming individuals. It is especially important to do so when they have a bad attitude.

Not only will your employee's inferior attitude effect the rest of the team. You will start to promote a culture of acceptance for underperforming individuals. At this point, performing representatives will no longer see the advantage of working hard for the company. By rewarding underachievers, there become zero consequences for not hitting your quota. Why would someone work hard if the company's stance on failing is that it's not only tolerated but rewarded?

Whether it be the inability to staff, HR protocol or simply the emotions of management getting in the way of letting someone go. It is crucial to your job security to get rid of anyone showing a pattern of missing their quota. This communicates a message to everyone on the team that a lack of performance is unacceptable to the company's culture. The termination of these individuals will create greater job security for a leader as the rest of your team will have a better understanding of their own responsibilities when someone is terminated.

Triple-A Candidates

There is not a single major league baseball team without a farm system to bring up ballplayers as needed. The Triple-A team is the ball club closest to the majors. When a player is called upon, they'll be there for the next game and are anxiously awaiting this promotion. Sales leaders have a Triple-A team of their own and are constantly farming this team for elite resources should these individuals become needed.

The concept is simple, obvious and talked about in numerous business books. But the job security segment on the Leadership Wheel cannot be achieved without a Triple-A team. Leaders do not exist if they have no team to manage. Hence, a leader will take care of their safety needs by following the ABI rule.

ABI – always be interviewing

A leader will interview two people per week even when they are fully staffed. Their team will take notice as this will indirectly apply pressure to the current sales reps. As they interview these individuals, they articulate the story and statistics of their green grass to create the excitement of the opportunity for the candidate. They are not looking for Double-A or Single-A players. They are only looking for Triple-A candidates to immediately add to their team when needed.

While there may not be an immediate roster spot, these top candidates are, typically, not looking to jump to their next position. They are interviewing you and your company at the same time you are inquiring about them and their background. This puts the leader and the candidate on a similar playing field.

The leader will express there is not a position open and accentuate their desire for the candidate to join them once there is. Knowing their own statistics, the leader will have an accurate timeline to supply the candidate. It will vary between companies and industries, but one to three months will typically keep a candidate on your Triple-A team if they are excited about the opportunity.

Once you've signed a ballplayer to your team, it's all about regular contact. In-person meetings are best to ensure you lock in your next hire. You should be attempting to buy them coffee or lunch every two weeks to stay in close contact with them. If you ignore them, they will seek a different direction where they feel wanted and appreciated. Correspondingly, you should be sharing something about the excitement of the team, company or an article on the industry by text, email or phone at least once a week.

Integrating them into the culture of the team prior to officially hiring them will provide your candidate with a platform to skyrocket once they officially start. Triple-A candidates will want to go on ride-a-longs with your sales professionals as an opportunity to shadow a day. They will request material on the company, product or service to study prior to coming on-board. You should make all of this available to your top candidates. And don't hesitate to demote someone to Double-A if they don't show interest in the materials or doing a ride-a-long. Triple-A candidates will have you itching to create a spot for them during this process. When possible, you should invite your candidate to a scheduled team event once there is an agreed upon start date.

Leadership Candidates

Sales representatives who you involve in the hiring process should be appreciative for the exposure. Reserve this activity for the employees that have the ability to grow into a leadership position, or, at minimum, a mentoring role. This provides them with insight to a next step in their career. Remember, they are looking to create their own job security as well.

When a leadership candidate has the opportunity to elevate their position, it is important you do everything in your power to help them take the next step successfully. A leader's legacy is built by the additional leaders they create. Multiple leaders will inevitably do substantially more than one. Are you growing your leadership presence by helping others do so as well?

Leaders accelerate their top individual's growth within the company. They are not looking to hold them back, and the other members of the team see this. This incentivizes the entire team to water their grass at your company. By propelling careers forward, everyone benefits. The team will continue their elite success as new representatives embrace an environment of promoting from within.

In a similar fashion, there are individuals more interested in staying in their current sales positions. It is equally important to provide them with growth opportunities. This could mean monetarily, a greater work life balance, mentoring others, or simply taking their knowledge to an expertise level. These sales experts are recognized by all, including the executives of the company. It is essential to know which direction your leadership candidates are looking to take.

Immediately take a look at the top two candidates on your team for careers in leadership. Itemize a plan to expose them to the opportunity they are seeking and start sharing more about your role. Provide them with opportunities to run team meetings, mentor new hires and get involved in the hiring process. You'll find this to be an intricate part of your job security as you create a culture of promoting from within through learning and growth. List your leadership candidates below and show this page to each of them during their next one-on-one to start or continue your conversation on growing their careers in the direction they choose.

1. _____

2. _____

8

A Room Full of Geniuses

Hiring is the most important thing you will do as a leader. Hire right and it will set you up for success. Prior to moving on to Requirement 3 of our Leadership Wheel, we are going to address the importance of hiring top talent in this chapter. This is the most crucial portion of creating job security as a leader to achieve the Requirement 2 needs of the Wheel.

I have been set up for successful travel in Cyprus; I have friends to visit and am familiar with the area. I decide to set myself up for another prosperous venture on my way back to Estonia. Since it is impossible to get to Tallinn directly from the island, I am going to Istanbul for three nights, where I can then get a non-stop flight.

I chose this location because a close family friend, Ismail, is from Istanbul. At minimum, I believed he could advise me on sites to see and things to do. It turns out, he is able to do much better. He is in town visiting his mom for an extended stay while I am here.

Ismail's kindness has brought me an entirely different experience to my travels. I hired the best possible candidate to learn more about the city. Ismail grew up here and is able to provide me with more information than the average tourist would ever know. I have been taken out to an amazing dinner, learned a few Turkish words and given direction to see parts of the city I would have never discovered on my own.

Multiple Candidates

If I had gone to a different city, I would have inevitably had a much different experience. But hiring one perfect candidate is not the solution. Your top candidate may fall out. This is the importance of the Triple-A team discussed in the previous chapter.

I have another friend, Nicki, who used to live in Istanbul. And while she is no longer living there, I reached out to her as

"Build a big Triple-A team!"

well in hopes that she would provide me with tips on the city. Not only has she provided me with a document of fun details on what to do, where to go and foods to try; she was able to coordinate an evening with her former roommate.

Ayfer is a nurse and has worked almost the entire time I have been here. But she is able to show me a few of the local bars with her friend, Ceren, during her one free evening. Between Ayfer and Ismail, I have learned one word well, "Şerefe!" This means "cheers" in Turkish.

Nicki's suggestion to meet Ayfer has provided me with an experience to make me feel like an Istanbul local. While the last thing I am searching for on my travels is any type of relationship, I try to never ignore a strong connection. It's there for a reason even if you never see the person again. I am going to stay in touch with Ayfer and update her on my travels along the way. Maybe our paths will cross again.

Traveling is obviously different than staffing your sales team. But they are both worth the time investment, whether it's a new relationship or employee. There is inherent value to having friends in multiple countries as you travel, and it goes far beyond having someone to play tour guide.

On a sales team, your production will go down when you are not fully staffed, and this situation could significantly damage your job security. You may have an elite team able to pick-up the slack. But there is no leader who will intentionally operate short-handed. Make it your mission to never put yourself in this situation.

Hiring the best possible candidates should be your top priority. If you maintain this indispensable activity, you will consistently have an Ismail or an Ayfer willing to show you around the city. If you continually source, interview and strengthen the relationships of your Triple-A team, you will find you can grow your job security to a level of infinite safety.

Triple-A Math

There is a math equation for the necessary size of your Triple-A team. Take your total team members and divide it in half. If you have 10 sales professionals on your team, you will need a Triple-A team of 5. The math is quite simple. Under normal operating conditions, you should not see greater than a 20% turn of your employees in any three-month period. A typical conversion rate on a Triple-A candidate is 40%. Remember the necessary work required to secure these candidates for your team.

For this example, you should be prepared to turn two sales professionals every quarter:

10 Current Reps x 20% Turnover = 2 Terminated Reps

From your Triple-A team, you will have your replacement hires:

5 Triple-A Candidates x 40% Closing Ratio = 2 Hires

Note, while you may have a strong relationship with each member of your Triple-A squad, your closing ratio will not be 100%. Top candidates are in high demand. No matter how well you operate the situation, your Triple-A team can and will look elsewhere even if you have an immediate spot on your team.

The numbers in this break-down are estimates taken from research on outside business-to-business sales. Established companies and teams may only turn one individual per quarter or even achieve no turnover during a quarterly stretch. Your situation will provide different hiring requirements, so it is important to know your math. Regardless, it is safest to recruit greater numbers in preparation to elevate your Triple-A team as needed. The best strategy is ABI: *Always be interviewing.*

Find Smarter People Than You

By hiring correctly from my own Triple-A team, I had an amazing experience in Istanbul and am now on to my intended destination of Tallinn. It's a Tuesday morning, and I arrive early to the Parliament Building of Estonia. Taavi Rõivas's advisor, Ave, greets me past the security check and gives me a tour around the building prior to sitting down for the interview.

Similar to my interview with Carr, I want Rõivas to concentrate on a leadership trait that he feels had an impact on his career and contributed to his success as a leader. Resembling my first interview, he is quick to respond. "The best leadership quality is to surround yourself with a great team of people who are often smarter than you." Often leaders are afraid of too good people on their teams. Trying to avoid this thing, because perhaps somebody is outshining you."

His answer is open and honest. Often times people think of leaders as the smartest person in the room, but this is something Rõivas is trying to avoid. By creating the best possible team, it elevates what could be done for his country. He isn't interested in formulating a team to simply agree with his own ideas; he is interested in advancing growth in Estonia.

"The best leadership quality is to surround yourself with a great team of people who are often smarter than you."

"My experience is the best team you can put together, you should. And it is very rewarding to work with a great team." It is apparent he isn't only talking about his enjoyment of the teams he's worked with. He is directly talking about the elite success created from these teams.

The Estonian government feels it is important to provide each citizen with the ability to access and gain information from the internet at all times to create an environment of learning and growth. Years prior to our interview, the country established the internet as a human right. And growth is what occurred. Internet access everywhere in the country became a gateway to allow residents to vote online. While this may seem like a crazy idea to most countries, Estonia set out with a task force to launch this as a necessary means to provide remote residents and traveling residents the ability to cast their votes.

Rõivas was one of the advisors for the person who decided Estonia should vote online. He explains Märt Rask's vision for Estonians to be able to do anything with their digital identity. "If you can securely identify yourself over the internet, you should be able to not only sign things, not only get services, but also to vote, which sounded like the most extreme thing to do with a digital identity."

By trusting in smart people, in 2015 every third vote was cast online. "We're a small country. We can't afford embassies at every village and town. So, it's rather logical if you are on a vacation or if you study in Finland; it's extremely easy for you to vote. You just need an internet connection and a secure I.D." It is easy to see Rõivas was surrounding himself with smart people. By forming an elite team, Estonia is advancing in directions other countries are not.

Similar to myself having more than one contact in Istanbul for successful travel, I learned Estonia prospects outside of their country as well. While the country's education program is well-recognized as farming elite talent, they still invest to have additional ICT students at the Universities. Rõivas detailed Estonia's own Triple-A team for me. "As it takes some time to get from high school to become a software engineer, we have also tried to do our best to attract people from other countries. For example, Ukraine and Finland have been the biggest groups of people who have come to work with us." The search for top talent is required to surround yourself with smart people.

Elite talent will inevitably produce elite results. And the experience Rõivas describes continues to share this sentiment. "I trusted smart people for the first year in the job of Prime Minister. One thing that actually came out of this was e-Residency. This was a crazy idea some people came up with. And they said if we introduce e-Residency, meaning providing the same digital identity to those people that are not Estonians, then we can make our country so much bigger, in many ways virtually, but also in terms of providing services to foreigners starting companies here."

Becoming an e-Resident of Estonia gives people out of the country the opportunity to apply for a secure, digital residency. If their application is successful, e-Residents obtain a digital identification card with a chip similar to those of Estonian residents. The card then allows the e-Resident to use Estonian public and private sector services along with resources. It also allows them to sign documents online and encrypt files. They would essentially be able to operate like a resident of Estonia for business purposes. The e-Resident would be able to open a business, a bank account and sign necessary documents remotely. Essentially giving people the opportunity to run and operate a global business, virtually, in the trusted European Union.

While the idea was radical, Rõivas trusted in his people and believed there was huge potential. Estonia is the first country to offer e-Residency and (at the time of this interview) has more than 22,000 e-Residents. These e-Residents have started more than 1,000 companies in the first year of e-Residency. Rõivas is proud of the success of this program. "If you trust those smart people on your team that have a great vision, even if it sounds unrealistic—especially when it sounds like something no one has done before—then you might end up with a huge success."

Elite Teams Are Built by the Triple-A Team

My interview with Rõivas illustrates several points on leadership. But his largest contribution to the Leadership Wheel is his determination to surround himself with the best people. By utilizing the best talent available, elite ideas are presented and achieved. Voting online and creating an e-Residency program

A leader's ability to source top talent will build greater team success over anything else they do.

were radical ideas, but these elite achievements were created by a team of top talent. There were no Double-A or Single-A team members making the cut.

As a leader, elite success is created through your team, not by the leader. Therefore, the largest contribution a leader can make to their own success is seen through those they hire into the organization. While every leader has the ability to coach and develop those on their team, you are immediately put at a disadvantage when forced to hire outside of top talent.

You will require a pool of performers to interview and hire when needed. Above average pay and benefits will afford you the opportunity to sit down regularly with the talent you are searching for. But all situations require outside of the box thinking to find the talent you seek.

Estonia is committed to fostering elite candidates through learning and growth. The country's education system, remarkably teaches some children to learn coding at seven years old. This constant investment in growing and sourcing top talent illustrates the importance of elite teams being formed prior to a candidate's first day. A leader's ability to source top talent will build greater team success over anything else they do.

You Can't Do Everything

Rõivas has done an eloquent job of detailing the importance of being surrounded with elite individuals. And it strikes a chord with me and my travels. I have failed to surround myself with anyone to assist me on the numerous tasks in the production of this book as well as on social media and the videos I am shooting to detail my travels and interviews.

Thus, the interview has gone well, but the filming has not. As a consequence of needing to travel light (*pun intended*), the use of professional lighting gear has been compromised. Unfortunately, we didn't have a lot of options on where to conduct the interview. And Rõivas's office does not have the best lighting.

I had two options: Interview in relative darkness or use an LED spotlight to give us a strong shadow. I decided it was better to see the interview, and the shadows would be my compromise. As someone constantly striving to achieve success at an elite level, I'm embarrassed at the quality of the video. I, myself, need to trust smart people to handle the video production for my future interviews.

After the interview with Rõivas, I have decided this will be my last book where I travel alone. I should be trusting smarter people than myself for tasks outside of my writing. Please go to GrassIsBrowner.com/press and watch the entire interview with our shadows. It's a great interview with an immediate lesson on the need to surround yourself with an amazing team.

Prior to moving on to our next chapter, make sure you've done the math on how large of a Triple-A team you will need for your job security as a leader. If you have achieved this number, you are not done. Triple-A members get recruited to other ball clubs, so you must constantly be looking to grow this team.

Finally, as we learned from Rõivas, you must surround yourself with the best and smartest people. Keep searching for those top candidates. You should be interviewing a minimum of two people every week even when you are fully staffed. If hiring is the most important thing you will do as a leader, you need to allocate appropriate time to be successful at it. Leaders wake up to a schedule. Take time to put the following three items on your weekly calendar and make sure you stick to your plan. Your job security depends on it.

1. Source candidates.

2. Interview prospects.

3. Follow up and meet with your Triple-A team.

9

Solitude Island

When I was working at a start-up in Silicon Valley, I hired remote workers because we were scaling quickly. One of my hires was an American from Atlanta, Georgia, now living abroad in Tbilisi, Georgia. The irony is not lost here. Mike is a sharp guy and eventually became one of the leaders of this remote team. We've stayed in touch over the years after we both moved on to new endeavors.

Hearing of my travels for this book in Europe, Mike reached out to make a case for adding himself and Tbilisi to the adventures. While I feel confident it will lead me to another concept for the book, the search for my family history has already taken a back-seat. I need him to line up a leadership interview if I am going to add another detour to my schedule.

Requirement 3: Network

Mike utilized his network to coordinate a meeting worth one final delay on my family search. So, I am now on a flight from Tallinn to Tbilisi for my third and final interview of the book. I am introducing the third requirement of the Leadership Wheel through my network and friend, Mike Holmes.

A leader striving for elite success requires a vast network which immediately starts with their direct reports. This segment provides a good example of how the Wheel and leaders are constantly changing focus, even when the lower requirement needs are not fully achieved. No matter what segment requires building on the Leadership Wheel, you are able to build your network today.

Your network must start with your direct reports, and the impact is far greater than meeting someone in a foreign land. Referrals for your next Triple-A candidate will often come from your team. As your eyes on the ground, the intel from your reps is invaluable to strengthen the company, service, processes, partnerships and product. The best ideas typically come from the field, and it is crucial for you to have a trusted relationship with your reps to gain this insight.

The driving force for leadership is being able to provide learning and growth to the careers of those on the team. This is a concept we continue to establish, repetitively, throughout the entire book as the center of our Wheel. No one wants to work for someone that doesn't care. And it is impossible to care for an employee when you are not providing learning and growth to their career.

Personal conversations of care often circle back to the employee's goals and ambitions in their career. While this is what leaders focus on to help individuals achieve greater reward in a comfortable environment, leaders naturally care for their people on a personal level because they are investing time and energy into them. When the effort is put forth in full as a leader, it becomes improbable to not have a personal relationship with the individuals on your team.

This will often make hard conversations harder. But leaders will never allow their personal feelings to get in the way of proper business goals being achieved on the team. If you are struggling with these conversations, I suggest you use the following word track:

"You know I care about you personally, but we need to address a few items from a business perspective."

Everyone understands this sentence. This is not an attack on someone's character or an attempt to tell someone you are no longer friends. As a leader in the company, you are required to push results and have a fiduciary responsibility to do so. Use the above word track or a similar one to establish your need to have a business conversation with your employee.

Due to these necessary conversations, the relationship between yourself and your employees must remain professional. But it should not detract from the personal connection you have with your

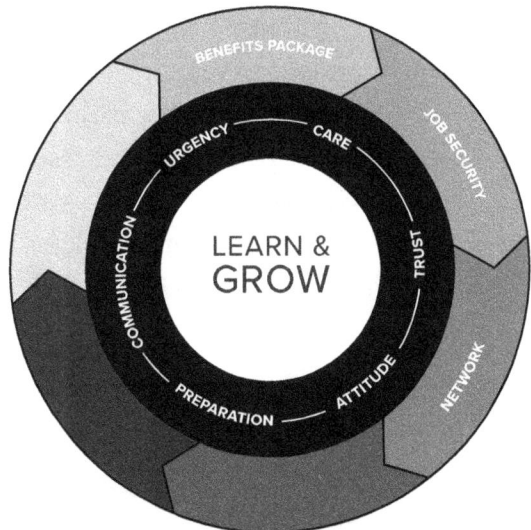

team. While this part of your network will not be built with your best friends, it will form close bonds with mutual respect and honesty.

Network with Peers

Every leader in a company is well-networked both internally and externally. This is another difference between leaders and managers. A manager will feel the need to do everything on their own and operate on an island. Do not make your home on Solitude Island. If you only have confidence in yourself, you will inhibit the overall progress of your team.

I have always believed in the philosophy of Robin Hooding top ideas. This means you should be networking with top performers to be in a position to hear about and replicate best practices. Like Robin Hood, you will borrow from the rich and give to the poor. Elite ideas are universal. Meaning, if a best practice is working well for a team on the other side of the country, it could be the exact thing one of your representatives needs to catapult their selling career.

The most important network for a leader is with their peers. There are ramifications for not building a network amongst your peers and endless rewards for doing so. There is no need to reinvent what works. The problem with sales managers operating on an island is they don't know when something already exists, which will cost them time and production.

If you are well-connected with your peers, you will be granted access to meeting agendas, structured blitzes and best practices working for other teams. While sales is competitive, the entire company profits through additional revenue. As a result, you are able to create sharing as a social norm with your colleagues when you build this network.

The people who have contributed most to my leadership career would be considered my competition. This network of peers can provide you with your next hire, mentorship and often be the catalyst of a promotion in your own leadership career. You should be looking at your peers as resources.

When a company has a conference event for their leaders, you should not be talking to the individuals you see on a regular basis. Please don't misinterpret this message. Of course, you'll want to spend time with the people you have an established relationship with. Some of them may be a vital part of your current network and influential to the success of your career.

The message is to not limit yourself to established connections. You would never want your own sales representative to stop networking or prospecting because they are content with their pipeline. As a sales leader, you are still in sales. Do not be content with your network. Grow it for your team and career.

ABN – always be networking

As you continue to grow your peer relationships, you will eventually grow your network to a place where you are always in the know. If there is a best practice working for a team or individual, you will have a peer sharing it with you. When there is a new partnership or program being implemented, you will be one of the first to hear. The list goes on, but the concept and importance of your peer network goes far beyond having a beer with someone in the same position as you.

If you are looking to grow your team to an elite level, you need to become the Mayor of your position so everyone includes you in their advancements. Success breeds success, so make this part of the cultural norm for conversations with your peers. Seek out the top performers and add them to your network.

You never want to miss out on what's working well. You'll find your role gets easier when you seize each opportunity to Robin Hood best practices. Now, you don't have to create everything on your own. If you expand on what's been given to you, don't forget to re-share. This network creates a mutually beneficial situation for everyone involved. And it allows each of you to concentrate more on hiring and coaching your people.

Network with Upper Management

As a sales leader, you should never treat everyone on your team the same way. This concept is followed by upper management, meaning your statistical success will be a large factor in building this network. Your relationship with upper management is an important one and provides you with different contributions to your leadership career.

In a sales organization, you should discriminate based on performance. In a culture of rewarding achievement, you'll find it pushes you and your team to succeed. Your network with upper management will stem from your quantitative results. This is how you are performing from a pure numbers perspective. Upper management cannot form close professional ties to a leader unable to hit their quota.

This does not diminish the qualitative interpretation of you and your intangible contributions to the company. In most environments, your personal relationship will weigh more than your performance for decisions that may benefit you. If there are two sales teams performing above quota, upper management will most often turn to the manager they trust and have a relationship with. This will provide new opportunities and advantages to the leader they qualitatively consider to be part of their trusted network.

I've spent my entire career enlisting for additional roles, which created significant work for me. If there was a regional conference, I was the first to volunteer and take on the largest speaking role associated with the meeting. If there was a regional task to contribute to each sales professional and peer leaders, I would raise my hand to do it.

Leaders looking to grow their careers take the initiative on additional responsibility to gain knowledge. This urgency to learn and grow in their own careers creates greater exposure to pass on to their people. From personal experience, I learned that upper management believed I should be recognized for my competence over the other sales leaders. The rewards often come in various forms. It may be an increase to your salary, additional sales leads, the opportunity to work with a strategic partner ahead of other teams or piloting a new program or product for additional revenue.

Do not take on these additional tasks solely because you are expecting a reward. A solid network with upper management takes time. As you take on supplementary projects, you are providing yourself with your own necessary learning and growth. Be cognizant of the fact that you are cultivating your own green grass as you invest in your career.

If you grow yourself into the most knowledgeable leader at your current position in the company, you will alter the perception of upper management and your sales individuals. You want your team to be working for a leader they feel operates at a higher level than their rank. Even when you are the head of sales, your commitment to learning and growth will dictate how this concept flows through those you both directly and indirectly lead.

Furthermore, conflicts with sales policies occur. At minimum, you'll be able to calmly explain your version of the story to a willing ear of upper management. You've earned the right to be heard. When you are able to make a fair case for your situation, you will be rewarded on a greater basis as there are gray areas to sales policies. All leaders want to recognize the person working hard when they can. When appropriate, you should use this to your advantage if you've built the right network with upper management.

Helping your representatives in conflict situations builds loyalty. Do not let the disputes become emotional for you. You are there with the presence of everything being fine. And you do not need to win every time something is brought to you. When there is a true discrepancy, it is most important your representatives know they are being heard.

Network with the Executive Team

The executive team at a company has the final say on sales policies, strategies and determines the implementation of new products, services and partnerships. Correspondingly, your ties and connection to the highest level of your company will position you with the ability to influence. This means your impact at the company is far greater than the average person. Your peers and sales professionals put high value and trust in your opinion. You may not be an executive, but you have direct connection to those making vital decisions effecting everyone in the sales organization.

While the members of the executive team can impact your career, you are necessary for their knowledge of the active and inner workings of the company. They are seeking the information you have as much as you are working towards providing it. Respectively, leaders operate on an executive level even when they are not. This means part of belonging to this network requires you to think like an executive. Sales managers are only concerned about their own world and look at things on a micro level. You must think on a macro level for the company.

While some of your communication with the executive team may directly benefit your current team or career, developing this network will occur by conversations geared toward growing revenue and decreasing costs for the entire company. Each one of your ideas and solutions to better the company should fit into one of these two categories. You will need to think about how the change will affect the entire company from a profitability standpoint.

For example, I was part of a pilot launching the first centralized CRM tool (*Customer Relationship Management*) for a Fortune 1000 company. Navigating without one profitably for the company's existence had the executives looking at the investment as an expense—this is why the pilot occurred. They were looking to gather more information on exactly how this would be seen as a profitable venture to the executive team, board of directors and stockholders.

It's not about one sales professional who wants to use Salesforce.com to schedule all of their follow-up because they used it at another company and think it's cool. Too often sales managers get wrapped up in the emotions and urgency of their team. They make requests to upper management and executives based on a promise to an individual. Do not be this sales manager. You must think of yourself as an executive and decide if the request has merit for profitability on a global level. The sales leaders able to do so will gain trust with the executive team and build themselves into this exclusive network if they show continued reliability.

"Maybe I could use some help?"

Network with Internal Partners

Internal networking for a sales leader should not be limited to the sales organization. There are other vital relationships to impact your career. Your network with operations, your recruiter and training department are all crucial partnerships for the success of your team and career as a leader.

Over the course of my career, I have watched sales managers fight with these internal partners or even ignore them rather than build a relationship. While you may sit on opposing sides of the fence for issues with operations, a leader who has a solid relationship with this partner will find solutions faster than one who does not. There is no reason to create additional bumps in the road when you are striving to build an elite team.

The same can be said for your recruiting, administrative and training departments. Remember, these departments have a devotion to helping serve you and the members of your team. You should assume they are coming from a good place. But, remember, leaders will forge a relationship so they can comfortably have business conversations and push progress when needed. It's easier to take constructive criticism from someone in your trusted network over a complaining sales manager.

The networking you do internally as a sales leader changes the dynamics of your team. Through your internal network, your team will start to see a pattern of being first. They'll be the first team to know about company information, changes, best practices, have the best content for meetings, have the latest articles on the industry and company. The list goes on.

If you operate your sales team on an island, your team will be stuck screaming for help. The benefits of your internal partners will be endless. You'll discover more rewards as you grow your career with your internal network. You may even end up making a few close friends along the way.

Network with External Partners

The most vital networking as a sales leader must be done internally. But external partners can change your course of success overnight. Appropriately, leaders are constantly fostering external relationships. However, this becomes secondary to the need for networking internally.

We address it here, so you are aware there is no stopping point to the networking of an elite leader. Your internal partners provide a long list of relationships to foster. And as we'll discuss later, your external relationships will be a driving force to elite success. Your networking should never cease in your dedication to building the entire Leadership Wheel.

Prior to moving on to our next chapter, take a look at your internal network. Have you formulated solid relationships inside your company? If you haven't, it's not too late to build and strengthen your connections. List the top three people inside your organization requiring greater partnership. Schedule informal meetings with each of them for the following week to discuss mutual goals and aspirations. Most important, have fun growing this network as you build relationships to contribute to each other's success.

1. _____

2. _____

3. _____

10

Taxi from Hell

The previous chapter detailed the vast network required for Requirement 3 of the Leadership Wheel. However, it does not address the fact that these relationships may inevitably be hard to form. There is often hesitation by sales leaders, upper management and executives to let someone new into their inner circle. And while I had someone in my network in Tbilisi, my initial connections did not go further than one.

Georgia is located where Eastern Europe meets Western Asia. The area is often referred to as Eurasia. And whatever you like to call it, I am having a hard time fitting in. I am in another country with yet another language I don't speak. And English is not prominently known. It feels obscure in most of my attempted conversations. In the previous countries I've visited, someone could at least fumble through a few words.

In Georgia, I am having everyone's head shaking no when I say the word English. And especially when I want to ride in a taxi. Money is a universal language though, and each taxi driver wants it. I am never sure if they know how to take me where I am going, but I am consistently motioned to get in the cab.

I am headed to Mike's house to hang out for the afternoon and see his place. His wife is cooking us dinner, so I am starting to feel my network expanding in Georgia. My stomach is about to be thankful.

Prior to my travels, I learned my cell phone carrier did not operate in Georgia. My communication while here has to be done through Wi-Fi. I have more than adequate instructions as Mike advises me to have the taxi driver take me to the Wendy's in Digomi. He is meeting me there so my travels in his direction will go well.

Digomi is a small area outside of Tbilisi, and Wendy's is a popular fast food restaurant in Georgia. Still, before climbing in the taxi, I confirm the driver knows the location.

"Wendy's Digomi?"

He nods his head yes both times I ask, quickly growing frustrated. He motions for me to get in the cab. His reaction and body language give me the impression that this is a place he knows well.

But a mile into the trip, the driver starts talking to me in Georgian.

"Wendy's" and "Digomi" are mentioned a couple of times, and these are the only words I understand. By his new tone and hand motions, I can tell he does not know where he is going. He sounds upset to learn that I also don't know where to go. He must have believed I could point him to my destination, which is nowhere close to accurate.

I tend to find this type of situation humorous as I do my best to see the positive. Quite often we find comedy in these events when we look back and tell the story. But rarely do we enjoy the actual moment. In this situation, I am doing my best not to laugh.

I can't even communicate to this man that I know how to find the Wendy's about as well as I can find the lost city of Atlantis. I keep repeating, "I don't know" and shrugging my shoulders to no avail. At our first stop, he yells through his window at another taxi driver.

With great relief, the other driver appears to point him in the right direction. We make a left and drive another half a mile. He pulls into a random parking lot. There are two men sitting in chairs as if they don't have a care in the world. My taxi driver yells loudly, disrupting their peace. "Wendy's!" "Digomi!" I appreciate his determination to find the place.

Poor Communication = Poor Network

It appears we have new directions to get me there. As we start driving again, I know I will be late and feel bad to keep Mike waiting on me. But I am embracing my own *Grass Is Browner* philosophy and enjoying the unusual moment. I am learning an interesting lesson on problems due to lack of communication. I am on my own island with no one to help.

Your network in the business world is required for knowledge you do not have. Without connections, your tasks can become immensely harder and take twice as long when you aren't able to communicate with the right people. Knowing this, I am appreciative of this man's determination and persistence to get me to my destination.

I feel sorry for the taxi driver as his anger continues along a remote road, and it becomes clear we are lost again. It's apparent he is living with a *Grass Is Greener* philosophy, and I can see how uncomfortable it is making his life. At this exact moment, he wants to be anywhere other than driving this American to a hidden burger joint.

He drives another half-mile, then pulls the car over to a small newsstand. He yells out the window with zero response. This lady isn't going to yell directions from her store. He makes a motion and says something to indicate he wants me to wait. This is unnecessary as it seems comical to me that I would be going somewhere. I have no idea where I am, and if he can't find this Wendy's, how could I navigate myself by foot?

He gets out of the car, slams the door and walks over to the woman. After two to three minutes, he is back. This time, he drives me straight to the Wendy's. He looks so proud as we pull in. He's been quite upset driving me, so I want to pay him extra for his determination—and get out. However, Mike hops in the car before I can say anything. Thank goodness, Mike is able to point directions the remainder of the way to his house. I don't want this poor man to have a heart attack!

Your Network Builds Your Network

Not speaking Georgian is an interesting hurdle to have in building an elite network. But by not having a specific skill, I'd created an intellectual barrier. The good news is, skills can be learned in the business world and in life.

Force yourself to learn new skills and be the most knowledgeable leader in your current position. This will allow you to reverse the network building process. At a certain achievement level, people will be approaching you to be part of their connections. And these new partners in success are able to bring you into their established networks as well.

Prior to building your skill set, you must leverage any relationship you are able to make. My network of one in Tbilisi has expanded after meeting Mike's wife, Kate. And Kate is the one who helped line up my final interview. Kate is close friends with Nona Mamulashvili, who has recently been featured on the cover of the Georgia *Forbes* magazine. *Forbes* had designed a special edition of the magazine in Georgia to put women on the cover as a way to inspire and promote successful women in politics and business. I love what *Forbes* is doing and can't wait to talk with Mamulashvili.

Mamulashvili is the head of corporate affairs in Georgia for an American Fortune 500 company. She is also serving as an Associate Professor at the International Black Sea University. Her background includes the public sector as the Senior Advisor to the Analytical Group for the President of Georgia, as well as political analyst at the Ministry of Foreign Affairs of Georgia. It's easy to see why *Forbes* picked her when showcasing a successful woman leader.

Your Skills Build Your Network

I am on my walk to the interview location on this sunny Tuesday morning. We decided on a coffee place close to where I am staying. And despite the short distance, I am leaving early to assure I won't face adversity on my travels to this nearby destination.

Mamulashvili arrives shortly after and with coffees in hand, we begin our discussion. We start talking off camera as I prepare her for my, usual, first question. "What is your greatest leadership characteristic that has impacted your career?" She states simply, "I enjoy facing adversity."

This short response peaks my interest greater than any interview answer I'd yet heard for this book.

"Throughout my career, I have consistently faced the stereotype associated with being a younger woman. People are expecting me to be the secretary or an administrative person for the meeting when I enter the room. Now as someone on the cover of a recognizable magazine, I hope to abolish this perception and inspire young women in the business world."

I am inspired by her goal and can see the fulfillment in her quest. I respond, "While age, color and creed should have nothing to do with success, they often become some of the biggest hurdles many face."

Mamulashvili is not alone in her challenge to build relationships in her professional network. She is not missing a skill for her work but stereotypes are real and people form judgements with them. And these situations will often become more challenging than my experience of not speaking the Georgian language.

I hit record on the camera and Mamulashvili provides her response to the stereotype she faces during our formal interview. "I stopped being angry, because I got used to people's reactions to me. I let them stereotype me until the moment they understood my strengths. This has become a game for me now. Because as I enter the room, people don't take me seriously. You may even hear a sexist joke as they are no longer serious about the meeting."

I appreciate her response. When someone is mistreating you from any stereotype or prejudice, you need to be courageous in order to achieve a *Grass Is Browner* philosophy

I let them stereotype me until the moment they understood my strengths.

on life and your situation. Mamulashvili loves the role her stereotype is allowing her to play. But it took time for her to develop this outlook.

"Because at first, I was angry when I was received in such a way. Then I got used to it. Now, I'm enjoying it. Because now when I go into the meeting I know what to expect." This may be a frustrating situation for most, but the moment is all we have. Mamulashvili is choosing to enjoy the excitement of changing the perspective of everyone in the room through her knowledge and skills.

She describes it as a game, and it is clear to be a game she is winning. "The first stage of the meeting they are lost at seeing a young woman in a position where an elder man should be. Then they think that I must have got there by chance. And then we start to talk. They eventually realize my looks are quite deceptive. They finally see the determination, knowledge and experience. And I observe how the tone is changing. It's amazing!"

Mamulashvili is tackling this prejudice as an opportunity to broadcast her talents at an even higher level. She needs to be at the peak of her game to disrupt the stereotype she feels as she walks into a room. "Some experiences are hard. But you learn to live with it. And at some point, you start to enjoy it. Because you know, in the end. They will treat you like they would treat any other (successful) person. This is not their fault they are stereotyping. Society has created those stereotypes and they cannot avoid it."

She is choosing to see the good in people assuming the worst in her. It is not surprising based on her background and success. You may be facing a stereotype of your own and can identify with Mamulashvili's story. There are many who will allow these perceived beliefs to limit them as leaders. It can hold individuals back from growing their network within the company. While there are no doubt various forms of unfair prejudice people face, choose to have fun with it and demonstrate your skill set. If you accept the challenge and grow your knowledge to a peak level, you will start to enjoy the game.

Some situations may not produce a fair result. But you can always choose your attitude on how you approach it. It may even require you to have a positive attitude as you change your lawn to gain a fair opportunity. But Mamulashvili's decision to have fun with these situations is a great example for us all as everyone reading this book will face a form of perceived unfairness during various points of their career. Choose to view it through the *Grass Is Browner* philosophy as we learn from Mamulashvili here.

Your Perseverance Builds Your Network

Most situations will not switch immediately. Especially in the eyes of a stereotype or prejudice. Perseverance is required in sales, and it will be required for you as a leader. Your urgency as a leader must extend to growing your knowledge and demonstrating your peak performance each day as you grow your network.

I am determined to not give up growing my connections, especially since I still need to navigate my way through Tbilisi. It is my last evening to grab dinner with Mike, and one of his friends is joining us. Determined not to be late, I am not leaving an internet connection until I take a few pictures on the map of where I am going for dinner. If I zoom-in on the streets of the picture, I shouldn't be back in the same situation. It seems like an obvious solution to my previous issues.

I walk to Freedom Square where it's easy to grab a taxi. I lean into the first taxi and show the guy my phone, asking if he knows the location. As I look up at the man in the driver's seat, I realize it is the same driver as the day before. In a city of over one million people, I am shocked to see this man again.

Without prejudice to my money, he quickly motions for me to get in the vehicle. The map must have given him confidence that he wouldn't get lost this time. Despite the terrible experience for him yesterday, I paid him well, so we are off and running to my new location.

We aren't even a quarter of a mile into the trip when he motions for my phone so he can look at the map. I hand him the phone, but immediately lose confidence in him getting me to my location. I can tell he, once again, doesn't know where he is going. And with his request to see the phone a third time another half-mile down the road, he starts to get upset.

This time it isn't entertaining to me; I don't want to be late two days in a row. Furthermore, I feel like I was lied to. I didn't get in the car until he saw the map. Since he has the street names and the exact location, I am frustrated to be back in the same situation.

By the time he's driven me to the general area and asks to look at my phone again, I decide to pay him and get out of the vehicle. I will take my chances finding Wi-Fi and figuring out the location over the angry taxi driver. And I, thankfully, arrive on time for dinner.

Your Trust Builds your Network

I vow to never get in a car with this taxi driver again. He is not someone I would ever want in my personal or professional network. I feel like he lied to me, so I do not trust him. Trust is required in leadership and in building your network.

No one wants to network with someone they do not trust. And breaking this trust will subtract from relationships you've already formed. It takes longer to gain recognition than it does to lose it. As fast as you can gain people to expand your network, it will subtract quicker under untrusted leadership.

"No one networks with someone they don't trust."

Everyone is at a different stage of their leadership career, but no one forgets what it is like to be a first-time manager. When your skillset is lacking, be honest with where you are at. I am honest with my lack of Georgian. If I were living in Tbilisi for an extended period of time, I would take a class and increase my language skills to improve my ability to grow a Georgian network. But whatever situation I put myself in, I would never tell someone I know where something is on the map if I don't!

Your honesty, skills and urgency to build your network will be the driving force in building Requirement 3 of the Leadership Wheel. Don't get frustrated during the process and maintain your intellectual honesty. We can all learn a great lesson from Mamulashvili. Enjoy the challenge and alter how people look at you through perseverance and knowledge.

If you believe you are facing a stereotype preventing the growth of your network, please write it below.

———————————————————————————

Now, draw a line through the prejudice you are facing. This will not be a limitation to your network or career. You will overcome it through the lessons learned in this chapter. This may not occur overnight, but you will keep working at it until it becomes a game you enjoy.

11

Flight from Heaven

I have an early morning flight out of Tbilisi to finally start my family journey. I wake up excited because my flight includes an overnight stay in Istanbul. And while I'll only be there for one night, Istanbul is a place I've wanted to visit again. Ayfer and I have been staying in touch since my departure from Turkey. And upon my arrival, we will explore the Princes' Islands together. It's a destination that I didn't get to on my previous trip, and she is, once again, excited to play tour guide.

I am eager to see her despite the longest passport control line I've ever stood in. Two hours later, I am on my way to meet her. It's a fun reunion as we arrive simultaneously at our ferry to the islands. We talk, joke and laugh the entire ride there as we pass through three islands before our final stop on the big island, Büyükada. As we arrive at our final destination, I learn there are no cars on the island. Our options to get around are by foot or horse and buggy.

We start our adventure walking along the cobblestone streets as the horses trot by. Everywhere we walk, there is an incredible view looking out at the sea. Later, we take the horse ride to a restaurant on the other side of the island. The sound of the horses leading our way float us back to a simpler time.

As many will attest, time moves fast when you are enjoying your company and location. I find myself feeling regret for not scheduling additional time in Istanbul beyond my one night layover. We've had fun exploring the island together, so I am disappointed to be headed back to the airport so quickly. In the moment, I am happy to still be talking and laughing with Ayfer as the ferry pulls away from the island and slowly gains speed.

After a long embrace at the Atatürk Airport, I keep my attitude positive as I think about my next destination to Prague. I am finally in route to the closest, large airport from the letters my grandfather had received for so many years in Poland. But what ended up being a sad goodbye took an interesting turn. I am two hours early for my flight, and somehow the airline doesn't have a seat for me. I am instructed to go through passport control and wait on standby for the flight.

I have zero interest in waiting for a flight without a ticket. I decline this offer as I understand the amount of time this would entail for me to go in and out of the terminal should my standby ticket not come to fruition. I haven't come close to forgetting the previous day where I stood in the never-ending passport control line.

After speaking to a manager, they agree to let me wait outside. If the ticket pans out, they will escort me to the front of the line. For my immediate future, I will be waiting one hour to see if everyone checks in for the flight. If I am, truly, bumped from the flight, they will put me on a plane the next day and compensate me for the inconvenience.

The minutes seem like hours as I let Ayfer know I may be able to stick around another night. We talk of dinner plans and where we could meet. Time flew by when we were together, but now it is moving at a snail's pace as I wait to get my answer on whether or not I will be staying.

Back at the service desk, I am notified that everyone checked in for the flight. I have to be the most excited person Turkish Airlines has ever seen to have their flight delayed. Not only do I want to see Ayfer again, but I am being well taken care of by the airline. They are putting me up in a hotel by the airport, paying for my dinner, giving me new flight arrangements the next day and providing monetary compensation for my troubles. I smile and thank each customer service rep multiple times for their generous resolution.

Ayfer and I meet at our new location for dinner, wine and more laughs on our surprise evening together. The only downside is that we have to say goodbye again. But, now, our conversation has changed to a discussion on where she can join me later in my travels.

Requirement 4: Recognition

We learned in Chapter 6 about the first requirement of the Leadership Wheel compelling you to work for a great company along with a product and service you believe in. If this isn't present, you won't be able to build the entire Leadership Wheel. And it is evident in our Turkish Airlines example.

Leaders are constantly thinking at an executive level. They are processing what is best for the company, the employees and the customers. Turkish Airlines illustrates this concept well with my delayed flight. While it is best for the company to overbook the flight for their profit margin, they did not fall short on taking care of their customers. By going above and beyond, employees are proud of their organization and have a better work environment. Instead of harboring furious customers, the service department was making it right for those delayed on their flights. And while

"Companies are recognized when things go wrong."

most people aren't excited for the inconvenience, I watched their customers respond kindly to being treated with respect.

In order to gain the recognition necessary for Requirement 4 of the Leadership Wheel, you must have a company represent you and your team in a way you can be proud of. The entire company benefits from testimonials of service. Not only are your customers happy, but they will refer and grow your sales numbers. As more happy clients are brought to the company, you are presented with more cases of recognition to share with your team.

This is necessary for your confidence as a leader of the company. But it is also required to positively highlight the company in interviews, team meetings and with your entire internal and external network. It is a crucial part of Requirement 4, which will only occur from this portion of your Requirement 1 needs being taken care of. Therefore, a leader needs to be at a trusted company.

Imagine if I was the only one to ever pay Turkish Airlines a compliment. This would not create much recognition for the leaders, the customer service team or any employee working for the company. Even those who do not function off of recognition need more than my testimonial video posted on social media.

Building an elite team requires recognition of the

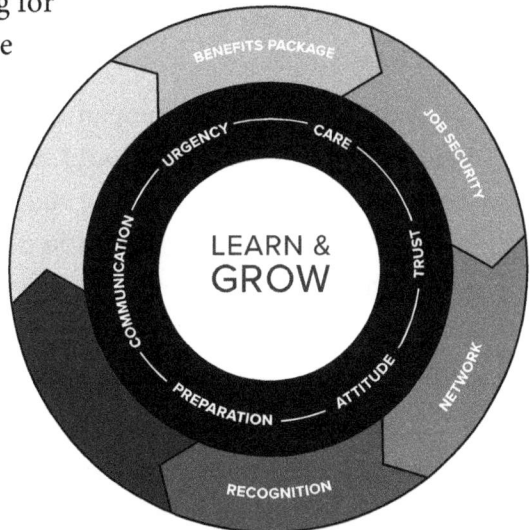

company's service. This will grow the sales numbers as a quality product and breed more testimonials as the clients come in. While the product or service may not fall into your direct responsibility as a sales leader. Leaders take initiative to increase the customer service level as they understand the impact it has on themselves, their team and the greater good of the company.

You are Customer Service

It has become too common in the workplace for someone to say, "That's not my department." This shift in responsibility and culture is not one you can allow as you strive to achieve your needs of this segment. Every employee in the company has a customer service role, because recognition will grow from service.

Top sales individuals take on a customer service aspect for their clients. They do not throw their clients to a 1-800 number when they are called with an issue. They get involved and make sure their company delivers on the service they promised the client. Leaders need to instill this attitude in their team as they lead by example.

While a majority of companies mandate a regular operations and sales meeting, you should have one whether there is a requirement or not. Your role should not focus on what this relationship can do for you. You need to narrow in on what you can do for the clients. This communication is crucial as no company wants to sell one product and deliver something different than what the client was sold.

I have spent my fair share of time in sales and operations meetings. The number-one mistake I've seen both sales and service managers make is their urgency to help themselves. This should not be anyone's agenda. The focus must be on the client; when this occurs, everyone wins.

If you are able to create happier clients within your company, sales numbers will increase. To do so, you need to consistently be answering one question while bringing suggestions to these meetings:

"How does this make the customer experience better?"

If you ask yourself this question, you are no longer in a debate on whether or not your query should be done. If it is good for the client, it is great for sales and operations. Now, it is merely a discussion on man hours and cost. The goal should be to implement the suggestions with the largest impact on the client's satisfaction. Once this is decided, it is simply a matter of breaking down the cost of implementation.

Sometimes the cost creates limitation for the company to move forward. Leaders will find a work-around for a lower cost when they have a relationship with operations. This is where collaboration occurs for the sake of the client in all circumstances. Looking at the situation through the eyes of an executive allows you to move past the idea if it doesn't make sense for the company.

You are Your Employees

When you are able to create a culture where the client comes first, you will have happier customers, employees and internal partnerships. The esteem of the company will provide great pride as testimonials flourish. Recognition as a leader will result from strengthening your product or service, but leaders gain their greatest recognition through their employees. There is no greater satisfaction for a leader than watching someone they brought into the organization achieve success.

You must be able to do the position of your employees to achieve their respect. There are sales managers who no longer know how to sell, which does not allow them to coach effectively. Not only have they not been on a recent appointment, but they may even lack the ability to roleplay the presentation.

Elite leaders are the best sales representatives on their teams. Not only is this required for new hires to learn best practices, it is further necessary for tenured representatives when requesting the leader's presence on sales calls. While a leader cannot spend all of their time selling individual deals, they are required to teach best practices for each member on the team.

Leaders must coach their team on how to sell, but a manager who focuses on selling individual deals will never achieve elite leadership. They are too busy selling to concentrate on the larger tasks for the team. Leadership is a multi-tasking act of hiring, training, retaining top talent and advancing careers with learning and growth. If you are not concentrating on these four tasks, you will fail as a leader.

Often times, selling managers do not create a big enough Triple-A team due to their need to help the team sell. Remember, the individuals you hire will affect your success greater than anything else you do as a sales leader. This does not take away from the fact that a sales leader must be able to sell.

Therefore, an elite leader takes pride in their sales skills. Schedule a one-hour block on your calendar weekly to work on improving your presentation and marketing materials as well as researching new articles and fine-tuning your own skills for your team. Based on your answers below, you may need to schedule additional time as you increase the quality of your presentation.

1. Do you want your team to emulate your sales pitch?

2. Are you coaching new practices to increase your team's closing ratios?

3. Does your team have updated marketing collateral and email templates?

Even if you answered the above questions in a positive manner, leaders provide a constant edge to win new clients. A sales presentation should never be stagnant. It requires constant growth to sharpen your skills. One hour a week is a minimal effort to add to your schedule.

Leaders take initiative on this type of project outside of business hours as they strive to build their elite team. If you are tight on time, pick a day to come into the office one hour early. If you spend an hour working on the three items above, you will see the value.

Build Your Business Plan

If your greatest recognition comes from your employees, you must build a business plan for your team and each individual. While the plan for your team is important to your own success, it will only work if your employee's goals add collectively to achieve the team's objectives. Therefore, it is important that everyone on your team achieve their own business plan as they stretch for optimal performance.

We learned how to calculate a basic business plan in Chapter 3. As discussed, it is an important part of the employee's first day. You want your new hire to understand what needs to be done to achieve their own version of success within the organization. But a business plan should not be done on the first day and forgotten. Too often companies put effort into business plans, meetings and programs where follow-up never occurs.

It's your job as the leader to push success for your individuals. Your employee won't be surprised by you holding them accountable because this discussion took place when the business plan originated. Remember, it is important your employee knows you will be monitoring their success.

The most important task to strengthen your current team is holding your individuals accountable. Given the choice, sales reps may opt to not learn and grow to achieve their stretch goals. If they are unable to execute their business plans, it becomes your responsibility to get involved in their calendar and monitor them to success. You know how to structure a day and week to achieve their desired results. If they've committed to an outcome, there is action required by both parties to achieve the goal.

We learned the break-down to calculate the number of appointments needed per week to get someone to their sales goal. But what if they are falling short of their objectives? If this is the case, no sales individual will be able to achieve any type of recognition by underperforming their activity.

Leaders do not allow their employees to fail. While sometimes a business plan needs to be adjusted to help get the most out of an individual, the execution of the goal is accomplished by a schedule. The solution to any sales equation is the activity. When it is not producing the desired result, more activity is required.

One-on-One

Despite the situation your representative is falling into, you are required to coach them to their goal. A leader takes the blame when success isn't achieved, and they will, likewise, give credit when it is. In a positive learning environment, the success should never go to the teacher. To assure you are able to provide this recognition, pull out their business plan during your representative's weekly one-on-one.

Each individual on your team should be on a weekly schedule. One-on-ones will vary across industries and company cultures. But for a productive meeting with your reps, please follow the seven guidelines below.

1. No longer than one hour

It is important to respect the time of the individuals on your team. Aside from a brand-new representative going through training, you should minimize the amount of time you are taking away from selling opportunities. Consequently, you need to be well-prepared for each one-on-one. You need to be on time and expect everyone to respond in kind. You should take disciplinary action for representatives not respecting time requirements for both one-on-one and team meetings.

Each portion of the one-on-one has a guideline for a maximum time in order to stay on task. This provides a reference as you establish what works best for your team. Total employee count may only allow thirty minute meetings for your schedule. Adjust accordingly to make the time as valuable as possible.

2. Start with a conversation (10 Minutes)

How is your employee doing? The answer and dialogue can be personal, professional or both. This should be kept to less than ten minutes unless there is a major event occurring in their life. Aside from this scenario, you should be ready to cut the conversation and let your representative know you need to start talking business to stay on schedule.

3. Follow up with company initiatives (10 Minutes)

This could include new policies, compensation plan changes, team programs, contests or projects everyone should be working on. This is crucial to keep everyone running in the same direction. Often times there are so many aspects of the sales job that company initiatives get pushed to the back burner. As a leader, it is important for you to care about what is significant to the company as well as the individuals on your team.

4. Discuss one to two appointments (15 Minutes)

You must discuss the rep's meetings on the previous week's calendar. This consistent process creates accountability in the documentation of activity. The conversation should typically be on "no sales" and "pendings." What happened and what coaching can you provide for this situation and future appointments of this nature?

As the best sales representative on the team, your knowledge needs to be shared. You are not perfect and will not close every sale either. But you are able to provide additional word tracks, ideas and best practices for your employee to implement after your discussion. Your job is to help them learn and grow. There is no better way than going through specific examples.

Having a one-on-one with everyone on the team allows you to share success stories from the network of your team. A leader is able to articulate best practices for any situation by consolidating their continued learning. Word tracks and alternate activity may be sited from around the country as you leverage these examples from your vast network formed in Requirement 3 of the Wheel.

5. Break down statistics (5 Minutes)

Provide an individual performance update with statistics for the week, month, quarter and year. This should be information you prepared for the meeting. This can be done electronically or printed out. I'd encourage these statistics to be publicly displayed in the office as it encourages a competitive environment. The importance is for each person to know where they rank on metrics you are measuring. No one should ever be surprised by their performance in sales. They should know how they are performing against their quota, teammates and company.

Sales representatives are competitive and are driven by stats. Make sure they know their closing ratio, revenue per unit, total annual revenue, appointments per week, and where they rank on these statistics. The data you are tracking may vary, but these would be the most common statistics for pushing results.

If they are deficient in any area, diagnose the problem. Do they need additional coaching on something more specific? Would they benefit from you or a tenured representative joining them on an appointment? Each representative deserves a minimum of two appointments with you per month no matter what their tenure.

Are you providing them with this time to invest in their development? One-on-ones will help dictate what should be focused on during these upcoming appointments. Make sure you schedule this time and do not alter their calendar or your own. Trust in leadership is created through expectations and follow-through.

6. Accountability (10 Minutes)

Further discuss their business plan and action items from the previous week. As seen above, this could blur into your review on their performance. Are they doing what they agreed to? What needs to be changed to stay on pace for their goal?

Provide specific action for the upcoming week and get involved in the structure of their calendar where necessary. Remember, the proper execution of the business plan is the responsibility of the leader. If the employee fails, the leader is to blame for not holding the representative accountable.

Proportionately, this is the most important time of the one-on-one. If this cuts into the final ten minutes of your scheduled time together, you should let it—you must hold your employee accountable for success. Push them towards their goal with, once again, no more than three action items if you are attempting to change their weekly behavior. When necessary, push the accountability to a higher level of inspection by creating daily check-in times to discuss activity.

7. What do you need from me? (10 Minutes)

Save ten minutes at the end for one question. "What do you need from me?" Your representatives should have this as an expectation if they want to discuss something specific at the end. This is important so they aren't interrupting the structure and flow of the one-on-one.

The only time this portion of the one-on-one should be compromised is when an individual isn't performing. This person needs you to hold them accountable and provide them with a structured plan to achieve success. They do not need anything else despite what they might be telling you. Use this additional time to push their accountability as you inspect every aspect of the failing rep's business.

As you can see, this is a tight agenda for one hour. Every leader has sales reps who love to talk and derail agendas. Provide a consistency of staying on task. It will require you to be well prepared for your time together. But, ultimately, your structure and coaching of your people will provide you with the greatest recognition a leader can achieve. You will directly impact the growth and learning of your representatives to contribute to their success.

Tenured Representatives

Performing representatives should graduate to a bi-weekly schedule as a reward. If you are conducting the one-on-one properly, these representatives may elect to stay on your weekly calendar. Others may not want any time depending on their tenure and success. Regardless, you should stick to a bi-weekly schedule for those requesting to opt out. This point pertains to elite sales reps as well. Use the time to take these high performing individuals to lunch and strengthen your personal relationship along with searching for opportunities to help this person continue to learn and grow in their career.

You'll find all representatives still need one-on-one time, even if they are telling you they don't. Be prepared for your meeting and quickly provide them with what you are giving the other members of the team. Share success stories of what is working. These insights will motivate your tenured reps out of a fear of missing out.

Even more important, top performers need their own recognition and are competitive. Make sure you have their statistics prepared. Update them on where they are at from a company perspective and their own business plan. If they have fallen behind, ask them if there is anything they've changed from their normal routine. Without accountability, even elite reps dull their skills.

You must provide new opportunities for tenured representatives to continue to learn and grow as they build their own careers. Get them involved in hiring new individuals, mentoring rookies, leading new programs and sharing their success stories in team meetings. Remember, their credibility on the team is greater than your own. Sales reps wants to learn from top performers. You'll find involving your tenured representatives in these types of activities not only grows the individual's career but strengthens the overall performance of the team.

This chapter is filled with information on how you can strengthen your relationship with your representatives and provide them with greater learning and growth to achieve success in their careers. This will be how you achieve the recognition necessary for Requirement 4 of our Leadership Wheel. The success of your individuals will create the accolades of your team.

Requirement 4 must be strived for by all leaders. There is no manager who has the right to ignore the responsibility of coaching their team to greater success. Whatever segment of the Wheel you are concentrating on, make sure you are providing your representatives with quality one-on-ones, conducting joint appointments and producing business plans with scheduled accountability.

While you may be working on mastering or improving Requirements 1-3 of the Wheel, you are still able to achieve high levels of recognition by properly coaching your people. No matter how incomplete your Wheel, every leader has the opportunity to directly impact the individuals on their team. Take pride in coaching your people. If you prepare and dedicate time to each sales rep, you will impact careers and lives. And this is the number-one reason why someone should pursue a leadership position in the first place.

12

Land of Opportunity

Self-discipline is required for leadership. A leader must be able to establish their goals and push towards them daily. The inevitable buzz of life cannot and will not deter them from their tasks at hand. Initiative will push you in multiple directions as you pursue elite success. But if you stay focused on building the Leadership Wheel, it will continually point you to what is required of a leader. And regardless of the turns you make, the goal of growing into an elite leader will remain clear.

The initial outline for writing this book was limited to three countries. My plan was to travel back to Cyprus, then trace my family roots in Germany and Poland. But I've completely altered my travels to the greatest needs in my pursuit of leadership concepts. By putting my urgency for the care of the book first, it pushed progress for the concepts we've read thus far.

Initiative has guided me into unchartered waters with each adventure contributing to our quest for leadership. While my plans have shifted to additional countries and experiences, I never strayed from the goal of searching for my family history. I don't want to leave Istanbul, but self-discipline requires me to maintain focus. I enjoyed the additional time with Ayfer, but my travels need to continue. Thankfully, this time I am able to get on my flight.

Prague is the best airport for me to affordably navigate to the small town of Lubań, Poland. Prior to World War II, the town was known as Lauban, Germany. The importance of this town is the belief that my great-grandfather, Rudolph Markwardt, emigrated from this German town with his father to the United States in the early 1900s, long before WWII.

My time in Prague is brief. I am fortunate to see some of this historic city, but I remain focused on continuing my travels. After my short stay in the Czech Republic, I head north on a train to Dresden, Germany, where I pick up my rental car and make the drive to Lubań. With limited hotel options, I opt for housing accommodations outside of the town from a couple renting me a room in their home.

My quest to see where my family came from is not necessarily an unusual one. The unconventional part is that I have little knowledge of our family history yet have decided to travel unguided by any concrete clues. Our immigration story is missing a number of pieces, so I am traveling to the one location my grandfather believes could provide me with more information. An actual town name was never communicated to him by his father growing up. But my grandfather's cousin, Eugenia, lived in the town of Lubań, where we assume my great-grandfather came from as well.

It has been ten years since my grandpa received the last letter from his cousin. In it, she wrote of growing in age, and her health failing. She told my grandfather that she was sad because this may be her last opportunity to write, and they had never gotten to meet in person. With no communication for years, my grandfather presumed his cousin's passing. He no longer had anyone to communicate with about his family's story.

The Markwardt Immigration Story

The immigration story I know is that my great-grandpa, Rudolph, came over with his dad, Adolph, at a young age in the early 1900s. Rudy, as my great-grandpa was known, came from East Germany with his dad to check out the United States and decide if they would stay here. As they decided to make their home in Minnesota, Rudy was left with German friends while his father went back to get the rest of the family.

This is, of course, an unusual part of my family's immigration story. While most immigrant families were moving to America for a new opportunity and life, it appeared our story was one of uncertainty. The entire family did not come on the first voyage, and they weren't sure if they would stay. Had my great-great-grandfather decided not to settle in Minnesota, the story would have ultimately been an extravagant vacation for the time.

Unfortunately, things did not play out as planned. Adolph was in a bad horse accident upon his return to Germany and later died in the hospital. Rudy was left in the United States, and his family never rejoined him. The story concluded with the rest of the family being sent to Russia. The details become sparse as communication was lost during much of this time.

It resulted in a story perpetuating a subject scarcely discussed. Rudy was a young boy waiting in a strange country for his family, but what tragically resulted was his father's passing. Then never getting to see his mom or siblings ever again. When my grandfather made attempts to learn more of the history, he reminisces of his dad's consistent response. "Some things are better off not talked about."

My grandfather was the only child and with Rudy passing in 1962, the family records did not go far. While we are unable to decipher when the first contact took place, we still have letters where my own grandfather was corresponding with his cousin in Lubań to stay in touch with these family members as best he could.

Despite the tragedy of my own family history, I am still interested in where my surname originated. I am proud to be a Markwardt. As I write this statement, I find it a little ironic. One piece of the family history is the confusion on the spelling of our last name. It is believed the family changed the "Marquardt" name to "Markwart" upon migration to the United States. The "d" was added at a later date to make the last name "Markwardt" because we were getting mail mixed up with a family of the same spelling.

Whatever the spelling, I am proud of my surname. I believe whatever the story, I am a descendant of someone looking for a better life. I am proud to be an American, and I am thankful for the advantages I have had growing up in my country. As someone who has traveled the world, I can directly see the opportunities I've been given by growing up in the United States.

Requirement 5: Elite Success

A leader cannot be considered elite if they are not managing an elite team. Requirement 5 is our most obvious need of the Leadership Wheel. An elite sales team is defined quantitatively by revenue produced or a percentage of quota. The status is reserved for the number one team in the company and larger companies may include the top ten teams.

It is not a segment a leader can accomplish alone. One will only achieve elite success through the individuals on their team. Appropriately, this requirement is, typically, only built after you've formed a successful team.

Building Requirements 1-4 on the Leadership Wheel results in team success and a greater amount of time for the leader with a well-constructed two-thirds of the Wheel formed. This provides leaders with an opportunity to re-invest their time and energy in the individuals on their team.

In our first chapter, we learned the first attribute of leadership was caring for your people. And this is an important element to revisit as we now detail elite success. It is not abnormal for a good leader to be content with a successful team. But an elite leader will continue to care by pushing learning, growth and results further.

To achieve elite success, you must have the foresight to provide the individuals on your team with greater opportunity than they ever dreamed possible. And the most notable aspect of this level is: a successful team gives the leader additional time in their schedule to provide these advantages to achieve an elite status. When a leader is scrambling to hit

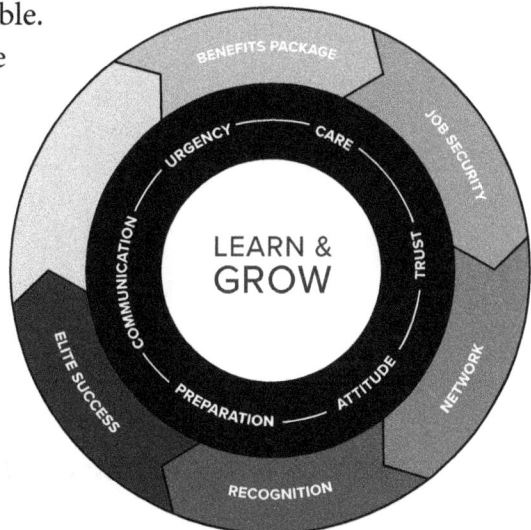

their quota or is understaffed, there is no way for the team to sell at their peak level. A leader's contributions are required for the benefit of each individual to collectively form elite success as a team.

The immigration story is a powerful one that parallels the pursuit of elite success. Rudy's dad was coming to America in search of a better life for his family. He cared to provide them with greater opportunities for the long term. While he may not have lived to see the extent of it, Rudy's descendants are living the American dream.

"Elite leaders provide greater opportunities."

Employees are the Priority

As we look back through each requirement in our Leadership Wheel, there are a few themes that jump out. Foremost, leaders put the individuals on their team first. They've invested their time and energy to make sure these representatives learn and grow their own careers to new heights. It is not hard to recognize a boss thinking they are above the team. There are many of them. A leader is able to create a culture of demanding a higher standard by making each individual the priority.

Leaders make you feel important and empower you to do great things. They do so by leading through example; they are not above the position their sales representatives work. In fact, they are constantly honing their craft to maintain the respect of the team as someone to emulate as they sell. And by doing so, each individual sees greater success as closing ratios and sales increase.

When you are doing the right things for your people, there is a high level of trust formed. It is no longer a hard task to hold someone accountable with business conversations. When the leader is trusted, an accountability conversation is often unnecessary. There is greater obligation and responsibility when working for a respected leader. No one wants to let down a leader they admire.

At the same time, no leader is perfect. Leaders recognize this and their own mistakes. This allows a leader's trust to never be broken. Consequently, humility becomes a supporting characteristic to trust.

Your team is not demanding you operate as a machine. As you care about them and your quest to grow their careers, your team will likewise care about you. Having an honest relationship with your people allows you to have tough business conversations. It further permits you to admit mistakes with insight as to what went wrong, so the entire team can learn and grow. This creates the open and honest culture necessary for a team to operate at an elite level with the desire to do so.

Freedom

As a leader, you can achieve greater strides to accomplish Requirement 5 of our Wheel once Requirements 1-4 have built the success of the team to its current status. Your team's trust in you as the leader is necessary to continue the team's growth to an elite level. The needs of the team are less than a team searching for their own identity. This accelerates the confidence in their leader; if they need something, their leader will be there when called upon.

A successful team comes with recognition and freedom, and the leader does not need to work as hard to continue their current rank of success. The leader has invested in their people and done the right things to build a successful team. At this point, various leaders may elect to enjoy their hard work. Recognition, higher income and a strong network of personal relationships are all rewards from realizing the first four requirements of the Leadership Wheel. Collectively, they often create contentment.

It is far more common to take your foot off the gas and set your team on cruise control. A great leader will still operate at a high level. They will continue to make sure their representatives enjoy their positions. They will keep everyone abreast of opportunities for learning and growth. And they will often participate in mentoring other leaders as they are featured on conference calls and meetings to share their insights.

These leaders are well recognized within the company and are typically happy in their careers and personal lives. And they should be. It is not easy to build a successful team. The joys of building a prosperous organization are vast. Furthermore, some people are uninterested in building their leadership career any further than their current position. It's possible, you've achieved the level of success you desire and your only goal is to maintain the culture and team ranking.

Maintenance

The easiest way to maintain your current status as a successful leader is to never get comfortable with the individuals on your team sticking around. For those ready to grow into other opportunities, help push them forward. Remember, you have a Triple-A team ready to be called on. Your next hire is anxiously waiting to be part of your team. Maintaining this successful culture is easier than creating it, due to the expectations of someone new entering the team. The individuals on a successful team will expect more from new members.

The energy required to be a part of this atmosphere pushes new hires to work hard and achieve results faster. This is not only great for your new hire, but it energizes the rest of the team. No one wants to be shown up by the newbie. Consequently, new ideas and competitive energy emerge.

We learned about preparing for turnover in previous chapters. While most people associate turnover as a negative aspect of leadership, elite leaders create positive turnover. This occurs when individuals on your team are growing into new opportunities within the company.

Positive turnover should be seen as an accomplishment of the leader. You are helping an individual's career grow and you are providing a larger contribution to your company beyond your sales numbers. A leader who cares about their people will see this as a triumph, rather than a boss's view of it as a potential hit to their paycheck.

Building the first four segments of the Leadership Wheel allows you to tackle Requirement 5 as a land of new opportunity. You can enjoy the fruits of your labor and maintain your status, which is easier than it was to grow your team to this point of the Wheel. In our next chapter, we start to take a look at how to build Requirement 5 of the Wheel, should you choose to do so.

If you have already accomplished the first four requirements of elite leadership, answer the question below honestly. There is no right answer to the question. There is only a right answer for you, your personal life and your career.

Do I want more free time, money or an opportunity to provide an even larger contribution to the individuals on my team and company? *Detail what you are looking to accomplish.*

_____

_____

_____

_____

_____

Whether you want to shift into cruise control or keep building the last two requirements of the Leadership Wheel, keep reading. These top segments are most often achieved by the individual efforts of a successful team. No leader would hold their team back, so your own growth on knowledge becomes equally important as we continue our adventure and explore these final requirements in the remaining chapters.

13

No, Nein, Nie!

The way you answered the question at the end of Chapter 12 provides you with a guideline for how to pursue action on our fifth and sixth requirements of the Leadership Wheel. Leaders have worked hard for their free time and larger commission checks, so their pursuit of the top two segments may not be with the same urgency seen in Requirements 1-4. Regardless of how you feel about tackling these levels of the Wheel, achieving the success of the first four segments gives you an opportunity to chase a new direction.

The inevitable rejection from building the top requirements of elite leadership often results in discouragement from a full pursuit. However, those looking to do so will embrace failure and let it guide them on the road to success. My current task at hand has me walking into a brick wall. I walk confidently though, as I am looking forward to what I might learn. The town of Lubań has a population of approximately 20,000. It is small, but I feel like it may as well be New York City.

The only lead I have is an address on a letter from ten years ago. And this was written from a lady my grandfather presumes deceased. But we believe her daughter is living there, which keeps me optimistic. While I am no detective, I am excited to follow my only clue.

My first day in Lubań seems to be a lost cause. I arrive late afternoon, so I shouldn't be expecting much, but I'm not off to a great start since I can't even locate the street on the envelope. I go to bed optimistic that I will find the address the next day with a better result.

I wake up refreshed, and decipher my navigational errors from the day before. This time, I make it to the street from the envelope. However, I can't find the house number. I park my car and start to walk back and forth. It appears the address is wrong or no longer standing.

I stop a lady coming out of a nearby building and use my phone to write my question in Polish while I show her the address and the letter. She speaks in Polish, attempting to give me a response. But without being able to understand, the conversation ends with her shaking her head. "No, nein, nie."

I have three forms of no communicated to me as it appears she said no in English, German and Polish to make sure I know she can't help. I attempt to ask a man coming down the same sidewalk shortly after, but it is a quick conversation. He only knew how to say, "No English."

There aren't a ton of people walking on this street. So, I feel fortunate to strike out with the two people I've seen. I have a feeling the building no longer exists. I walk over to the side street trying to find a matching number of the house on the letter.

The same man comes back out of the apartment building and gets into his car. I decide to wait for him at the exit of the parking lot and quickly type my question into my translator to explain that I am looking for a relative at an address on this street. Approaching the exit, I pull up my hand to say stop and hold up my phone. His curiosity gets the best of him, and he rolls down his window to look. He reads my message and motions for me to get into the passenger side.

He explains that he knows a few words in English and he will try to help me find the building. We drive to the end of the block, and he turns around. We repeat this process in the opposite direction with a final U-turn. As we return back to our original location, he points at a broken-down building being renovated.

I get out, thanking the man, and give the building a full inspection. Fortunately, and unfortunately, the right number is on the building. I won't be getting any answers from this stop. I decide to make my way back through the town and look elsewhere. After trying the city hall, the library and a closed museum, I eventually go to the city tourism center. I'm surprised there is a tourist building in such a small town; maybe they'll be able to help.

Luck Follows Hard Work

I am greeted kindly as I walk into the tourist building. The two women speak enough English for me to understand that they want me to wait. They make a phone call, and a lady named Anna arrives, shakes my hand and speaks with amazing clarity. "Welcome to Lubań." And with these three words, I feel relief and hope.

Anna and I go to her office. "What do you do in Lubań?" I excitedly ask.

"I am in charge of helping to market tourism for the town and write for the local newspaper." She flips the conversation by asking me, "What are you doing here?" And my long story ensues.

Not only is Anna fascinated with my response, but she wants to help me learn more. She orchestrates a plan to introduce me to the person in charge of the museum as he also serves as a local historian.

"He might be willing to research and help you investigate your family's presence in the town," she says. "We'll meet him tomorrow for a private tour of the museum, and maybe he will be able to uncover more of your history."

My first full day in Lubań feels like I've found moderate success. But, ultimately, I struck out on finding a family member, which would provide me with the greatest possibility to learn more about my roots. A tour of a museum with a town historian is great, but I came to find a relative to provide me with concrete answers.

When I get back to the house I am staying in, I attempt to do more research online. We know the names of my grandfather's cousin's family in Lubań. And prior to my travels, I'd looked on Facebook and Google searches to see if I could find any information on these family members. It seems like a dead end to look again, but it's been months since I've performed those searches.

Every search leaves me empty-handed except one: I have found a Krzysztof Kordas on Facebook, which is the same name for one of Eugenia's grandsons. Unfortunately, his profile does not indicate if he lives in Lubań. If I email him, I may come across as a complete weirdo. But this is the only search resulting in anything close to a relative. I decide to take a shot in the dark to find out if his grandmother is Eugenia.

To my surprise, I receive an email back from Krzysztof four hours later. He confirms that his grandmother is my grandfather's cousin. With continued fortune, he is living in Lubań with his wife. He asks if I want to come over to their house for dinner tomorrow.

One Sale Increases Production

The theme of elite success in Requirement 5 is for the leader to get their hands dirty. Whether it is writing an awkward email or picking up the phone, it's time for a leader to strike out as much as his own sales professionals. The sales reps are used to the constant rejection. It's part of the job, and they know each "no" is leading them to their next "yes." But in our first four segments of the Wheel, most leaders begin to no longer experience rejection the same way they did during their selling careers.

Despite still being in sales, the rejection of missing out on a sale does not impact a leader the way it once did when they were selling. Correspondingly, leaders start to enjoy the comfort of not experiencing rejection on a regular basis. This results in some leaders not being able to go back into sales. They've lost their tenacity and perseverance to deal with the daily brush-offs required to be an elite sales professional. These leaders will struggle with Requirement 5, because this is what's necessary to take your team to elite success.

A team needs their leader to advance past their own success. The team's full potential stems from the leader's involvement in providing additional sales directly to the team. The minimal achievement in this segment can start tomorrow for every leader. The question you need to ask yourself today is: Are you in sales? Every sales leader should respond yes to this question and immediately start selling.

The product or service your team is selling should be on your mind for sales opportunities the same as it is for your sales professionals. As you walk into businesses in your daily life and talk to friends and family members, it is important that leaders are prospecting their contacts for sales. Part of your life needs to be a solicitation of business to provide for your team.

When you are able to achieve a sale through your own network, you should take care of all the paperwork unless you want to use it as a coaching opportunity for a new hire. The

"Sales leaders sell!"

purpose of picking up the entire sale is to use it as the ultimate motivator for your team. Not all sales professionals are motivated by a gift card, corporate trip or celebration dinner. And, yet, this provides others with their greatest effort for these contests. But all sales professionals are motivated by sales!

Generating a sale of your own allows you to create a competition for your team to dictate the behavior you want to see from each individual. You can now give the sale to the person with the most appointments for the week, the highest closing ratio for the month, the most referrals, the most telemarketing dials and the list goes on. You'll find the largest enthusiasm for a contest is in direct relation to your ability to generate a sale.

It is easier for a leader to sell once a successful team is built, because they have more free time. This allows for the leader's own prospecting to be scheduled on their calendar. Thus, it will provide a further reach outside of their personal network. The leader may even have time to telemarket with their team.

When a leader makes dials during team telemarketing to generate appointments and sales, they become one of the team. You are in the trenches and fighting for the team's full potential. Not only will your additional sales improve the numbers, but it will motivate your team to push harder and do more than they otherwise may have settled for. If their leader is making dials, they can certainly hammer the phones to prospect additional sales.

One Referral Partner Increases Production

The same holds true to helping your team expand their referral networks. Are you actively going to outside meetings and mixers to look for top networking partners? Remember, you are a sales manager and in sales. You can't be above the process of an elite sales professional.

This concept gives you the opportunity to network for your team. I encourage all leaders to join a networking group and attend weekly. If you join a good group, this should generate at least one sale each quarter.

You may even find your next hire through the group or mixer you attend. It's all about what you share when you describe what you are looking for and what you do. Formal networking groups provide you with an opportunity to give a one-minute advertisement on your company each week to solicit the type of referral you are looking for. When you give this weekly commercial, use it once a month to let everyone know you are hiring and describe the benefits of working for your company.

Often leaders are not able to attend a networking group weekly. Let members of your team sub for you during the weeks you cannot attend. Provide this as a reward to allow them to work the leads coming in while they attend or promise them the next lead from the group. These opportunities should be reserved for team members above quota.

Quota is the Minimum

It is considered a best practice to make being above quota a requirement to winning any contest, being dispersed a new lead, given a new referral partner or handed an inbound sale. This establishes quota as a minimum to each sales professional's job requirements in order to partake in these benefits. There should be a higher standard on a successful team and raising the precedent will be necessary to achieve elite success.

As a countermove producing similar results, you could require being at quota to maintain territory size, referral sources and certain freedoms. Individuals not at quota may have these resources cut and dispersed to the individuals deserving additional responsibility. There may be extended telemarketing time or structured activities for those not performing.

The goal of motivation by subtraction should not be for punishment but for creating an environment of structure to aide in performance. Your job is to help everyone hit their minimums to achieve their desired pay. When an individual is underperforming, they are not focused on their own success. Subtracting resources allows a representative to concentrate on the activities providing the highest return on their time investment.

This subtraction example demonstrates how crucial it is to set expectations on the position and the anticipated income during the interview process, as we discussed in Chapter 2. It will allow you to come full circle without activities such as these coming across as hostile management. A detailed explanation using intellectual honesty will foster the support and direction for this individual to continue their plan for success.

No matter how well you set expectations during the interview process, it will, inevitably, create turnover when you treat under-performers different from the rest of the team. But an elite leader wants quota dodgers to start performing or leave. They will have their Triple-A team ready for anyone who doesn't want to play ball.

Even after you've built a successful team, it's still possible to have an outlier. Treat this person differently as you strive to take your team to elite success. This is all part of creating a competitive sales environment. An elite team will have everyone above quota and does not need these types of motivators. And this is what you are striving for to properly construct Requirement 5.

Exponential Sales

We've now discussed how leaders can provide additional sales and help drive their team to a higher level of production with their own sales abilities. This effort can be done by all leaders without regard to the current performance of their team. However, once Requirements 1-4 are achieved, a successful leader can take their sales process to an entirely different level.

My travel in Lubań is no different in the pursuit of elite success; I knew I would experience emanate failure. This did not and will not deter me. I've planned time in my schedule to run into road blocks, and my previous travels have produced an important baseline of success for stories and concepts of this book. I know if I only experience rejection in this town, it will still be an important topic for this portion of the Leadership Wheel.

Chasing down elite success for your team is no different. While you may pick up a sale or two with the beginning processes of this stage, elite success for your team is achieved by the leader's own failures in search of something far greater. This is what will propel the team to a new height it could never achieve on its own.

The truth of the matter is, my first two days in Lubań have been lonely. A small town in rural Poland has me stuck using my phone to translate my story into Polish as I scour the town for clues on my family history. Not only am I running into numerous dead ends, but the language barrier has a majority of the people not wanting to help because it's too hard to communicate.

Furthermore, history is real but often fades fast. You may be able to act as a great leader for years, but someone's perspective of you as a leader can change in an instant. You must constantly be striving for elite leadership. There is no end point on a wheel, and no end to your leadership quest.

On the day of my arrival in Lubań, I talked to a young man outside of a church that I was visiting in search of historical records. Fortunately, he spoke enough English for us to communicate. The young man questioned me on how I could be from Lubań. He listened to my story about being of German heritage and recognized my surname as German. I had to explain to him that where we were standing was once Germany prior to World War II.

While it came as a surprise to him, it did not come as a surprise to me. As humans, we often get caught up in our now. We don't take time to learn from our past, and we don't have the patience to properly prepare for our future. Elite leaders strive for both.

Elite success requires proper preparation for this future intention. Not only do you know you'll be met with failure, but you recognize that this segment may take a long time to achieve. Furthermore, those who chase it may never see their failures come to fruition. Elite success is just that—elite. Therefore, it is not achieved by everyone even if you are doing all of the right activities. But when it does occur, elite leaders create a legacy for their team as they often go on to alter company practices and policies.

For me, it is seeing months of preparation and research for my trip resulting in nothing more than an empty building and a museum tour. But a response on Facebook has the potential to change everything. I am attempting to achieve what would be considered elite success for my family by finding our untold history.

Prior to moving on to Chapter 14, it is important for you to recognize the gift that keeps on giving. One sale will not produce elite success for your team nor will it alter company dynamics. This stage is often achieved by a large national account, a franchise relationship, an exclusive referral partnership, automation to email campaigns, creation of additional lead generation facets or any type of efficiency created to give your team more selling time.

All of these examples provide an equation for exponential sales for your team, most commonly, created through an external network. It is important for you to develop your own hit list on what these opportunities might be; start chasing them once you've successfully built the first four requirements of the Wheel. Or, start today and find these opportunities now!

List your top five opportunities for elite success:

1. _____
   _____

2. _____
   _____

3. _____
   _____

4. _____
   _____

5. _____
   _____

14

Family Reunion

I'm having an interesting day in Lubań, learning about the town through a private tour of the museum, shown by the historian. He is a kind gentleman, who has committed to doing research on my surname. While it is a productive day, it all feels purposeless in comparison to my fast-approaching dinner with my relatives.

We are meeting at 5 p.m., and the minutes can't go by fast enough. Krzysztof's response to me on Facebook was in Polish, so I am wondering how our conversation will go. I have my computer and am ready to communicate with my phone upon arrival.

My grandfather's stories of communication included the hardship of getting letters translated. With the letters sent to him in languages he didn't understand, the task was arduous to find translators to interpret the sentiments and well wishes. Knowing these family members were to undergo a similar process to understand his messages, he was forced to keep the correspondence simple. Ultimately, he failed to learn our family history due to the communication barrier. Thankfully, technology has advanced and is giving me confidence that I'll have a different experience.

As I walk toward our meeting point close to the museum, I can see Krzysztof sitting with his wife, Ewelina. I wave, and they both get up and walk towards me. I'm feeling nervous about what our greeting will be like. Are they excited to meet me? Are they apprehensive to help me in my search? Do they speak any English?

I have questions with all kinds of possibilities running through my head. But they approach me with big smiles and hug me hello. While at times the world can feel lonely and huge, there are still moments where this planet can feel overwhelmingly warm and small.

I quickly go to my phone for translation. I understand our verbal communication is going to be a struggle. Technology allows us to determine that we are heading to their house for dinner. The communication is non-stop with typing and translating all the way to their home.

Krzysztof is driving, so Ewelina and I are typing; she then speaks my message to Krzysztof in Polish. It is a comical way of getting to know each other, but the entire car ride is filled with excitement and laughter.

In their home, the communication moves faster as I am able to use my computer. Krzysztof tells me my grandfather's cousin, Eugenia, is still alive. She is suffering from dementia, which has caused her memory to fail—which is most likely the reason my grandfather hasn't heard from her in so long. Krzysztof explains to me that she is out of town with his parents, taking a summer vacation. He contacted them when he got my Facebook message to confirm who I was. Knowing I am part of the family helped him meet me with confidence.

Wrong Town

I continue typing to explain my story and the search for my family history. At this point, things take a turn: I am not from Lubań. They aren't sure where my family is from, but they know it isn't here. Krzysztof is on the phone with his dad, trying to locate any family records he might be able to find. Eugenia was good about keeping the family history together, and they believe she might have something to help me.

Eugenia's house is close by, so Krzysztof leaves and returns with a large file of paperwork and pictures. We find my grandfather's letters and photos of my family he had sent to his cousin. It is strange to somehow be looking at my own picture so many miles from where it was taken. With great persistence and a little luck, I'd put myself in the right place at the right time.

Also in the file is a paper written in German that gives more details of my family history. Ewelina translates the message, which tells the story of my great-great-grandfather, Adolph Markwardt, venturing to the United States with his son, Rudolph Markwardt. Finally, the key piece of information I have been looking for!

Just as my grandfather has told me, Adolph returned to get the rest of his family and take them to the United States. This is where Adolph had the horse accident, and the document says he died three days later in a hospital in Russia. The story is tragic. His wife, Berta, took a rope to hang herself, but was stopped by the family from doing so. The unfortunate turn of events altered the course of the family, and they never went to the United States.

This archive went on to provide details of my great-great-grandmother, Berta Markwardt, coming from near Calau, Germany. Playing detective to put the clues together, I combine this new information with my past knowledge. The one piece of information my family knows is that we are from East Germany. Calau is a small town in East Germany and less than two hours from Lubań.

The information from my Lubań relatives and the new file of documents has provided me with three new pieces of information. Definitively, my great-grandfather was not born nor did he ever live in Lubań or what would have been Lauban, Germany, during this time. Secondly, the exact location of my great-grandfather's birth and where he grew up is inconclusive due to the reference of Russia in the story. Finally, the German document with the location of my great-great-grandmother points to my family being of German descent.

With basic reasoning, I make the assumption that my great-grandfather was born somewhere in east Germany, most likely near where his mother, Berta, was from. But this is only an assumption—Berta and Adolph could have moved to Russia prior to any of the children being born. And this would give me a new and larger country to search, where no city seems to be indicated on any of the documents from this time.

Prior to this dinner with my relatives, I thought I may come away with the information I was looking for. But by finding additional information, I now know less than what I previously believed. This new version doesn't provide me with definitive answers. But it does provide me with a lead. I will be traveling to Calau, Germany.

More Time Equals More Leads

I have worked hard for my new lead, but it may not produce a *sale*—or in my case, the answers I am searching for. This is the scenario of every lead as no one closes at 100%. But every sales leader knows giving more leads to their team should produce greater results.

At the most basic level of lead generation, you can provide your team with more leads by providing them with more time. If you are able to help them increase their efficiency, you can allow your team to do what they do best—sell!

The first part of building the opportunity for elite success on your team has everything to do with automation. It is important for a leader to constantly be looking to improve processes. This may mean something as simple as automating paperwork.

The first company I did sales for had me manually writing on multiple paper forms to sign up a client. The paperwork alone would take me a full hour to properly fill out and submit to operations. But the longer I was with the company, the more this process changed.

Eventually, I was typing information that auto-populated fields onto multiple forms. It resulted in only needing to type something like a company name once. And instead of walking the paperwork over to the operations department, everything—including the client's electronic signature—was submitted online. What once took an hour could be done in under fifteen minutes.

My selling hours were extended with paperwork taking less time in my day. And this is exactly what you want for your sales team. To achieve Requirement 5 of our Wheel, each leader must concentrate on creating greater efficiencies for their team. These types of new processes will not only change the dynamic of how your team operates, but they will often effect every sales individual in the company. And while each company is different for processes needing greater efficiency, your focus should start with the inefficiencies on your team.

This could mean you are creating or further customizing your CRM tool. I've seen sales organizations where a CRM is not even in place. This means each individual is creating their own system for follow-up on prospects and clients to upsell or solicit referrals. Consequently, turnover often sees leads disappear and current clients in the dark.

The end result of creating or improving a CRM for your team and the company is once again more time for your team to sell when using an automated system. This equates to more leads as they won't go missing during a transition. Automation can be taken a step further with email addresses put into a proper system. From an executive level, you are now able to launch follow-up emails and automated messages to new clients. Whether you are trying to reengage a customer, upsell a current client or solicit referrals along the way, the end result is more inbound leads for your sales team and the company.

Automate What You Can Control

Some leaders never take a look at creating a process of automation because they do not believe it is within their control. Regardless of where the company stands with implementing new practices, you can still create a more efficient method for your sales team. This results from your urgency and initiative. It does not come from an executive granting your wish.

As a sales leader for a company that was not producing follow-up emails for the current client base, I decided to write a monthly email for my team. The email provided educational material, highlighted an ancillary product and asked for referrals. The sales reps would manually email this to their client lists. A simple bcc to a few hundred clients resulted in referrals and upgrades that my team would have never had without this call-to-action in place. It wasn't optimized to the highest level of efficiency, but I operated it to the best we could at the time.

As the process produced results, I learned people outside of my team were using the template email. More teams were now operating with a greater efficiency and even more leads were coming into the company. While the movement wasn't as automated as it could be, it was more efficient than having each sales professional come up with something on their own each month.

Take the next ten minutes to pause and reflect on the efficiency levels of your team. Write down three practices you can optimize for your sales reps.

1. _____
   _____

2. _____
   _____

3. _____
   _____

While it is important to work on automation through your operations partners and executive team, this takes time and is often not in your control to achieve automation at the highest level. None of the items above should be dependent on someone else. This exercise is a process of dedicating your own time and energy to grow the productivity of your team.

When done properly, you will find yourself with a proof of concept to implement and automate companywide. Not only will this provide greater impact, but with corporate resources the process will be optimized to a peak level. As the theme of this segment reads, all of your efforts benefit the team with additional time. You will need your team to use it to capture elite success.

Swing and a Miss

You can achieve moderate success in Requirement 5 no matter where your team ranks in the organization. At the lowest portion of this level, we learned sales leaders need to sell. It's all about generating additional sales through your own efforts, additional referral partners and helping create a competitive sales environment where the leader is working with and for the team.

As you strive for impact on your team throughout this segment, we learn any leader can create greater efficiencies for their team. These practices can potentially impact the entire sales organization. Providing your reps with more selling hours in their day is a portion of Requirement 5 that will equate to growing your team success. But the upper echelon of this segment tends to provide only rejection to leaders, which does not equate to more sales. This higher level is, therefore, typically reserved for successful leaders having the time capacity to handle this without interrupting their team or day.

There are sales teams who achieve elite success with naysayers citing the only reason was because of _____. This in and of itself should have your attention. If there is a sales team achieving elite success by doing one magical thing, don't you want to do it too?

Because the result is so hard to achieve, most sales leaders don't bother "wasting their time." But swinging and missing over and over again is what brings you closer to connecting with the ball. You must have a structured schedule of swinging for the fences, or you will never hit a homerun. You are not wasting your time, because you are continuing your leadership quest with an already successful team.

Large Partnerships

Franchise relationships, national accounts, an acquisition and exclusive referral partnerships are all built through a long sales cycle. An external network of this caliper takes time to build. But the good news is it simply starts with one contact. You need someone in the right building to point you in the right direction. Persistence and time will allow things to pay off for creating a relationship with someone who can help you.

Most of the time, it does not mean these relationships will benefit you right away. It may take years before you get a proper meeting with the correct person. These big swings rely on a dedication to the process and a high level of comfortability with rejection.

You may need to spend an absorbent amount of energy to even get to the right contact and still end up with a swing and a miss. This corresponds to the key of success for Requirement 5—being able to swing as often as possible. Instead of chasing down one sale for your team, share what you are working on during a team meeting. Let them know the large national accounts, partnerships, acquisitions, and referral relationships on your hit list.

Two things will happen by sharing this information with your team. The first is someone may be able to further your cause. At minimum, these large swings are now on everyone's radar as there is a payoff for the entire team. The second is your team will continue to do their jobs at a high level because they know you are dedicated to the team's success.

New Heights

When one of your big swings connects, you'll find it creates a golden handcuff to members on your team. You've created the greenest grass on the block for your individuals and no one wants to go anywhere else. The excitement of the large opportunity elevates the current, green grass of your successful team. Everyone is making more money and the leads are at an all-time high, which creates a sales atmosphere of fun and excitement.

Make sure you are celebrating team success. We talked earlier about the importance of team events. As the team

Boss vs. Leader

"Employees benefit a boss.
A leader benefits employees."

performs at higher and higher levels, remember to reward, recognize and celebrate the accolades of your team. This adds to the allure of everyone, including yourself, enjoying Requirement 4–recognition.

While elite success is created through a culture without turnover, this stage will provide individuals on your team with promotions and new opportunities within your company. For those looking to expand their career, you should set aside time to help them write a business plan for the position and provide your insight to gain the promotion.

This is a counterintuitive approach to a boss. Bosses are selfish and only concerned for themselves. But leaders looking to build the entire Wheel concentrate on the individuals of their team without regard for self-serving purposes. Expanding the careers of the individuals on your team is necessary for achieving the elite success of Requirement 5 and starts to blend into the Requirement 6 needs of creating a greater good for the company.

As you develop a team with only positive turnover, you will find transitions to be smoother with the new person. Your former representative is grateful for everything you did in expanding their career. At minimum, they feel obligated to help make a smooth passage to your new team member.

Often times, the transitioning employee will put up big numbers before they leave as a demonstration of loyalty to you and your leadership. They have an exciting story to share as they target their hit list to announce their transition. Not only are they able to take a last swing at their prospects, but they are able to introduce the new person if the account doesn't close. This provides your new hire with a bigger pipeline comparatively to negative turnover.

Leaders grow people to new opportunities and relationships do not cease from company hierarchy. Regardless of the formal chain of command, leaders will maintain relationships. An elite leader's network is vast. And there is no greater person to have in this network than someone whose career you've directly impacted. Make time for these former employees and make sure they achieve success during this transition in their careers.

Achieving Requirement 5 is a special opportunity for the leader to do something more. Sequentially, members of your team will be rewarded with career advancements. Together, elite success has been achieved and gets noticed. Embrace and enjoy the success surrounding your team.

An elite leader's success is never in threat once Requirement 5 is fully achieved, because a greater distribution of leads will assist in the success of your team members. The excitement of bringing in a Triple-A candidate will reinvigorate your elite team alongside the inspiration of positive turnover. Your newest hire will work harder because it is required. They will not fit in if they are average. The team will mandate they perform at a high level, and they, consequently, will from the pressure of their peers. Thus, elite success will not cease when built properly.

An elite leader will spend proper time preparing for their own turnover. Upon achieving elite success, the leader often takes

Leaders grow people to new opportunities and relationships do not cease from company hierarchy.

on a promotion of their own. After all their hard work building the team, the last thing a leader wants is for it to be dismantled. Make sure you are grooming someone for your position as you get ready to take your own next steps as positive turnover.

Remember, this will be part of your next opportunity in leadership as you lead the sales manager of your former team. Prior to moving on to Requirement 6 to complete our Leadership Wheel, please write your top three candidates to take over your position. This is different from our exercise in Chapter 7 where you listed the top two people on your team to expose to leadership. Your replacement is not required to come from your team. But you should require your future hire to be the best candidate for this opportunity.

Create an action plan to properly expose these three candidates to portions of your position they may not be aware of. This should be done in coordination with your peers if a candidate works on an alternate team. But the purpose of this exercise is for you to have greater clarity on who your replacement should be. Stick to the exercise being three candidates even if you are confident on your anticipated successor. Elite leaders know not to count on anything or anyone being 100%. Furthermore, the candidates not hired on this list will join your new Triple-A team.

1. _____

2. _____

3. _____

15

The Funeral

My drive to Calau, Germany is only two hours, but my brain is on overdrive the entire way there. I've done preliminary research in order to figure out a few places to inquire for information. But I am back to flying blind with my only lead being a small town in East Germany with no one to talk to upon my arrival.

Furthering the confusion is the family record, which only specifies that my great-great-grandmother is from "near Calau" according to Ewelina's translation, so I may not even be going to the right city. There are two towns surrounding Calau called Lübben and Lübbenau. Both of these towns sound similar to Lubań, which was my original destination. Maybe one of these towns is the correct location.

Keep Swinging

I get off the highway and follow the sign for Lübbenau, where I stop at the tourist center. No one speaks English when I first arrive, but they call a woman to the front and Mia listens to my story. She interrupts me mid-sentence and exclaims. "Marquardt, I know that name." She goes to a computer and pulls up a website of a Marquardt funeral home on the main street of Calau.

"I think you found where I'm going next!" I am ready to run out the door after writing down the address. But with an English-speaking resource in front of me, I continue with my line of questions. Similar to the need of an elite leader to keep swinging, I need as many opportunities as I can find.

"Where are the historical birth records kept for the city of Calau?" Mia responds. "Hold on." She starts talking in German to one of the other workers and then shows me another website.

Three minutes later, I have an address where the records are kept for this region in Germany. Apparently, I can pay someone to research birth archives. It looks like I have more than one strategic, cold call added to my day. I thank Mia repeatedly and walk back to my car at a brisk pace.

My day couldn't be off to a better start. While the last place I intended to go during my travels is a funeral home, I am excited to say hello to a fellow Marquardt with my new lead. In my mind, even if we aren't directly related, we must be distant relatives. And I am sure they will be able to help.

I park my car in front of the town hall of Calau. The main street is small, but it is vibrant. People are dining at local restaurants and others are relaxing on the benches that line the street. As I walk, I see the Marquardt name on a red sign lining a gray building.

I walk past the building to gain my courage to go inside. The awkwardness of the situation is sinking in. "Hello. I'm your long-lost nephew from California." I need to come up with a better introduction.

I circle back and walk inside to be greeted by an older lady sitting at the front desk. "Hello. My name is Jon Markwardt. I am from the United States and I am tracing my family history." I hand her my German family document. She looks at the paper briefly and hands it back to me almost immediately.

"I'm sorry. Do you speak English?"

She responds, "No, and I'm busy."

I keep talking as it appears she understands, whether she feels comfortable or not speaking the language.

"I am sorry if I came at a bad time. But I've traveled a long way. Do you know any of the names on this document?" I hand her the document again and quickly receive it back. "No. We are very busy."

I feel like the deceased should be rather patient customers, but I am wrong. I have come at the worst possible time. I decide to leave as our conversation is going nowhere. I, defeatedly, grab a business card at the front desk.

I take a moment to compose myself at a local coffee shop. My "family cold call" could not have gone worse. As I'm drinking my coffee, I decide to look at the situation positively. Maybe the language barrier made her uncomfortable. I pull out my laptop and type her a nice email apologizing for coming unannounced and at a bad time. I translate my entire message into German, attach my family document and press send.

My search continues as I meet a woman at the district archives of Calau. Kristin takes the time to understand my entire story and agrees to manually go through the birth records, marriage records and anything else she could find on my family surname. She lets me know the dates I am asking for are not available as digital copies, so she will need to sort through the original archives to see if she can find anything.

The search will take time and she warns me not to be optimistic as these older records are incomplete. Since I am not certain of exact birthdates or if this is the correct location for any of my relatives, I am back to swinging for the fences. And I am well beyond strike three.

My day continues as I find a museum not open, a lady at a church who can't understand me and a closed town hall. I eventually stumble on another tourist center for the city of Calau. Here, I meet a woman named Renate, who is determined to help me.

Renate is able to communicate in broken English. And when she doesn't know how to say something, she speaks in German. The conversation takes patience, but one thing is clear: I found someone willing to help as she invites me into her car.

Since churches often kept birth records for everyone in the town, she brings me back to the church as she knows the lady there. With a quick conversation in German, I have another person who agrees to do research for me. This was a much different reaction to when I first met the woman.

As we drive to our next location, Renate continues to share pieces of Calau's history along the way. I am fascinated to learn more with the possibility of my family's relation to the town. We turn right onto an all grass, residential street. It seems like we are driving on someone's yard, but it is clearly a road as there are cars parked on it. We stop and get out of the car.

This is where I meet the local historian as we walk up to his home to greet him and his wife. He commits to conducting searches in the library. And four days later, he lets me know a Bertha Marquardt checked out a book in 1904. I was ecstatic as it gave me confirmation of my great-great-grandmother living in Calau, Germany! But upon further research from the church, it was determined this was a different Bertha Marquardt than the one I was related to. This, actually, didn't come as a big surprise as my great-great-grandmother's name is listed as Berta, not Bertha, on all of the family documents.

On the same day that I hear from the Calau historian, I finally get an email from the Marquardt funeral home. My patience in translating my questions into German nets me a response. She is kind enough to email me back and explain the relatives on my document were not shared by their family tree. Fittingly, this lead is dead.

Celebrate Wins Daily

Two of my biggest leads from Calau netted me zero results. But I deem my efforts a success. Renate had circled the entire town with me and expanded my search significantly farther than I could have ever done on my own. Shockingly, she was able to introduce me to all the right people in one day. As evening has come, I am invited to eat dinner with Renate and her friends before I travel back to Poland. I am appreciative, and the dinner tastes amazing after a long day.

Food, simple rewards and recognition are particularly important post hard work. They help us push onward and remind us an accomplishment has taken place. Sometimes we forget how little things go a long way. It's important as a leader to continually recognize and show appreciation for your people. It doesn't need to be a hit to your expense budget. Often times, a coffee or simply acknowledging hard work with a phone call or text message is all the employee needs from their leader.

Most people do not enjoy failure, so it's important to encourage everyone on your team. Just because someone isn't achieving immediate success doesn't mean they are performing the wrong activity. The process of things not going right for me, ironically, was still a process of enjoyment. I was having a unique experience and felt confident I was doing the right activities to find my family history.

While I am coming up empty handed, I am enjoying the journey. I am meeting amazing people that are helping me do far more research than I could ever imagine doing on my own. There is fulfillment in updating my parents and particularly sharing the news with my grandfather.

I call my grandpa from Poland to give him a full update on everything I am doing. I can hear the fascination in his voice from all the research and his interest in everything I found and didn't find. Sometimes we find answers without answers. The belief he'd had for years was his dad came from Lubań. While I hadn't found the answer, we now knew this wasn't true. Maybe this should have been frustrating, but for my family it was a glimpse into our past even though the view wasn't clear.

Getting a Sale Without a Sale

I am enjoying this process of failure as a shared experience with my family from afar. Not only is it fun to share the stories, but it gives me confirmation I am doing the right activities. Maybe I am not achieving the results I want, but the progress reports to my family confirm I am doing the best I can as I am met with encouragement and support.

At various points, my parents helped me research things online. They would search for cemeteries, city archives, churches and our last name of various spellings through towns of my travel. We are in this together and working as a team. By not operating on an island, I am able to enjoy each failure as I believe it will point us in the right direction.

Your leadership should operate the same with your team, because not getting the sale doesn't mean failure. This is possible by joining in on their process to help them grow in the right direction. To get a sale without gaining a new client will have various meanings across industries and sales professionals. For a new person on your team, their sale for the day may be learning their presentation or facts about the company. For someone struggling with telemarketing, it may be learning new word tracks and setting an appointment. If you treat the little victories as sales and celebrate them, the right activity becomes routine as new skills advance the results.

"I never worry about action but only inaction." In this famous quote by Winston Churchill, it details the importance of supporting activity in your sales organization. Hard work pays off, always. And when you've done the hard work to hire the right person for your team, you should support them as long as they continue to put in the necessary activity. Celebrate their efforts until you are able to recognize them for their success.

Doing the right activity will achieve success. This is a different matter if the person is working hard but cannot generate sales. As we discussed termination in Chapter 7, sales numbers inevitably educate the leader on whether or not your representative is doing the required tasks to prosper in their position. Support your hard-working sales professionals until the sales numbers no longer allow.

Requirement 6: The Greater Good

Requirement 6 is where high caliper leaders identify gaps to further build the company. This creates career advancement opportunities for everyone in the sales organization. The result is a greater good for the company reaching far beyond the team. These leaders contribute learning and growth to the masses as everyone in the company benefits.

In order to build this top segment of the Leadership Wheel, it is crucial we go back to the beginning of the book. The six leadership attributes establish our characteristics required for elite leaders. While each is necessary for achieving the greater good, preparation is the most important characteristic for this top-echelon of the Wheel. You must prepare your team with the right mindset for your people to be motivated to push for something greater after achieving elite success.

Preparation is required to accomplish each segment. But your team may struggle to build upon Requirement 5 of the Wheel without proper planning prior to their accomplishments. Elite success comes with its own rewards, and urgency may be lost with higher income and recognition. The best way to strive for something more impactful is to prepare for it from the start. And when this is done properly, an elite team has the ability to accomplish Requirement 6 at the highest level. With proper motivation and preparation, urgency intensifies with the elite success of a team. The goal is now in reach, and the team continues to prosper.

The greater good could have various meanings in the business world. And while it can be introduced right away, it can only be achieved in full by creating additional company opportunities to carry-on for generations. This ongoing benefit will impact the business, employees, customers or even an outside organization.

Bob Carr started our venture with his vindication of putting his people first, above all else. Not only is this a crucial theme throughout the book, but Carr introduced his own vision to motivate his employees to work for the greater good of his company. As you may recall, he is donating his ownership to a charity to help kids go to college, which might otherwise not have the opportunity. As the sales, company and profits grow, so would the number of individuals sent to college. Whether you identified with the cause or not, Beyond was founded with the principal that the leadership team would have motivation to produce a greater good for the company at its core.

This greater good goes outside of the immediate people on your team as it creates more opportunity for the entire sales organization. While this will vary by industry, teams and individuals, we look to Carr's example of starting with the motivation for Requirement 6 first. Carr is fostering an environment of employees inspired to build and create more and more career opportunities to grow the company. The greater the company expands; the more money is provided for additional kids to attend college. As a result, company growth and expansion occurred rapidly after their launch.

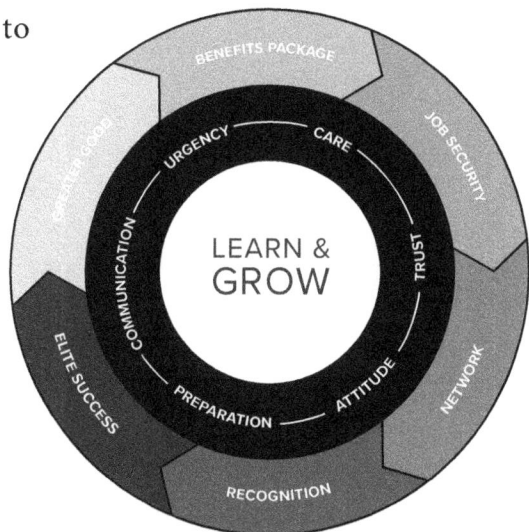

Bird's Eye View of the Leadership Wheel

While we have detailed the needs of elite leadership through a step-by-step process, it does not accurately depict how elite leaders develop. One must prepare for the entire Wheel from the beginning in order to achieve all portions of the Wheel. Therefore, elite leaders are constantly thinking three steps ahead. You must know where you are going to know where to step next.

As a leader in your sales organization, you must consider the bird's eye view. Where do you want your team to go and how do you want the team to look once they get there? How can you incorporate your own greater good plans for your team today?

While various start-ups and entrepreneurial ventures are realizing the business purpose of a noble cause, these leaders will ultimately fail if they skip out on the necessary components of the Leadership Wheel. Companies are coming to market appealing to the altruistic desires of consumers as a company having a mission to be something more. But if this mission doesn't include a vision to benefit their own employee's growth, the company

"Leaders plan for success."

will not withstand the pressures of a competitive environment without career advancement built into the organization.

Prepare Your Own Greater Good

Regardless of their mission, cause, monetary goals and ambitions; elite leaders will make their people the top priority. While a few leaders are able to build motivation for the pursuit of the greater good for the company from inception, the most crucial part is remembering the greatest asset of any company is their employees. Thus, the preparation for this greater good is outlined through a plan of the advancement of careers and lives for each person on the team.

Elite teams fight for this cause when the leader is not around. The motive is spoken about by the team first and the leader second. And it becomes a team effort to build and achieve this mission that does not fall solely on the leader. The goal in a sales culture is often to be the top team, but the mission can take on various meanings for career expansion and fulfillment.

Requirement 6 of elite leadership is where new corporate policies and procedures are born. And, ultimately, new career positions are created as the team, company and opportunities are enhanced. As elite teams do something different and achieve abnormal results, executives want to peak behind the curtain of what makes this team function different than the rest. This is where your sales goal and mission statement written at the end of Chapter 1 comes to fruition.

Once an elite team is formed, there is more time for creativity to enrich the sales organization. It now becomes commonplace for the individuals on the team to create greater opportunities for themselves and the company. As the highest performing team, they have access to greater attention to implement their own practices for the benefit of the company as they alter the structure of the organization. These changes will result in the creation of new career opportunities. You may find one of your team members as the new head of national accounts and another in charge of growing franchise relationships.

There may already be a greater good your team wants to fight for to help advance the company. But having the additional time and motivation to swing and miss will allow them to enjoy the process. Building new opportunity into the sales organization requires beta testing, proof of concept and a business plan. While these tasks mandate additional work without any promise of imminent change, it can and will be a process an elite team will enjoy. I hadn't found where my great-grandfather came from, and I was continuing to run into more dead ends. But I was loving my journey. What greater good vision would your team be equally excited to chase?

Plan a future team meeting to have your sales team envision being the number-one team in the entire company. They should imagine making more money, achieving great recognition and doing so on a more efficient schedule then they are today. Define this as the direction your team is headed and prepare for these results. Discuss what the team would like to focus on upon achieving this stage to greater benefit the company and what would motivate them to do so. The needs of the company are always best seen through the eyes in the field.

There should be no wrong answers to their vision. But the right mission will provide desire to create structural change for the company and a legacy around the team's elite success.

Striving for a greater purpose transcends selling to keep each of us moving in the direction of something bigger than ourselves. Define the team's mission which may be different than your own in Chapter 1.

_____

_____

_____

_____

_____

_____

_____

_____

16

Catching a Whale

The rest of my time in Poland went by fast. I explored. I wrote. I met up with my relatives for another dinner. And I finalized plans for the last leg of my trip to Germany. My research continued as I sent my fair share of emails, but I continued to swing and miss on every attempt to track down family records.

Throughout my travels, I continued to talk to Ayfer. And to my surprise, she purchased a ticket to Germany right before I left Poland. I was shocked she considered knocking on random doors in small towns a vacation. But she made it clear she wasn't concerned about what we'd be doing. Not only was she considerate of my agenda, she was genuinely excited to be a part of it. And so, Chapter 16 begins with a twist as I will no longer be traveling alone.

It is the last day of August as I awake to the night sky. I'd packed the evening before in preparation for my drive as I walk out the door to the quiet of an early morning. The sound of my suitcase being placed in the trunk is the only noise to be heard aside the methodical flow of the river next to the house.

I reflected on my time in Poland as dawn is breaking. Upon my arrival to Lubań, I had envisioned my great-grandfather as a young boy looking at the same sights and sounds I was hearing today. As I drove through the city one last time, I understood this town meant more to me than it could have ever meant to Rudy Markwardt. This is a town he had never known. But for me, I'd met new friends, found relatives and gained greater information on my family history. This was all done with a language barrier and relatively no concrete information upon my arrival.

A leader's past results will not achieve their future success. My thoughts shifted from reflection to where I was headed. While it is important to evaluate success and failure, it is equally important to know where you are going to push forward. I was headed to Leipzig, Germany as Ayfer would be arriving on an early morning flight. It is a three-hour drive and not far off my path for continuing onwards in my journey.

I arrive at the airport as Ayfer is walking out the door. "I can't believe you're here!"

She responds in a serious voice, "Neither can I." We both laugh and get in the car to continue our conversation.

It's a fun reunion filled with cautious excitement as I did not know what to expect. But with a clear agenda, we know where we are going. After a quick breakfast, we are on our way to Calau.

Recognize Elite Activity

Unfortunately, the church records did not find anything on my family. The local historian wasn't able to turn up any more information. And my paid research through the town archives netted zero results. With no success, I decide to make our first stop to visit Renate. I'd bought her a bottle of wine as a thank you for her kindness and help in my family research.

Sometimes a person can do all the right things and not achieve the desired results. This is especially true when they are hunting a large partnership or a whale of a client. To me, this does not diminish the activity. I often find myself with a greater appreciation for someone who goes the extra mile and doesn't get the results they deserve.

Are you showing your appreciation for your employees when they are excelling in their sales tasks? Activity will inevitably foster success. It's more important you concentrate on your team performing the right daily tasks to form long term habits. Short term results will only provide you with short term solutions.

It was a fun reunion with Renate. And Ayfer got a firsthand view of what our time would look like in small town Germany. We'd be meeting more people where we would continually fight a language barrier.

My search in Calau would be harder without any positive results from our previous activity. But Renate surprised me as she was still working to find something on my family. She'd found another business owner in the town with the last name of Marquardt. He owned a hardware store, and while we were visiting, she called him to line up a meeting.

Renate also knew a gentleman who was knowledgeable on tracing family histories. She thought he may be able to help and lined up a meeting with him as well. I was extremely thankful for her guidance and support. Outside of these appointments, we would be expanding the search to surrounding towns to cold call additional churches and town archives to provide me with the family records I was seeking.

My Family History Found a Greater Good

Renate helped me understand my cause was one she identified with and cared about. This was something she had chosen to

"Celebrate a good fight!"

work on when I was not around as the cause motivated her to do so. She went above and beyond the searches we'd done together during my first trip to Calau. As I reflected on the journey for my family history, I saw a pattern. While I was fortunate to meet many amazing people to help me, each one of them was excited about helping my family learn our history.

My friend, Anna, from Lubań found the story so uplifting she wrote about it and put me on the front page of their newspaper. Kristin from Calau's town archives felt so terrible she couldn't find anything that she looked more disappointed than myself when she gave me the news. And my Lubań relatives, spent countless hours looking through documents and translating messages in hopes of finding the answers I sought. And my list goes on for the numerous people who interrupted their days to provide assistance to my cause.

Looking back at my travels, I can see my search was personal to everyone I met. I wasn't asking for money to be donated to a worthy charity. But I was asking people to volunteer their time. With so many people motivated to help, it became clear my cause provided fulfillment.

A number of the individuals I interacted with told me of their own revelation on wanting to search for their family history. My story was one of inspiration. As my grandfather was getting older and time was passing, there becomes a point where it would be harder for me to trace the family history alone. This fear of giving up one's history was motivating others to follow a similar journey for themselves. It's possible that you, the reader, may even take it upon yourself to research and greater solidify your family tree.

As my cause was creating opportunities for others, we use my family search as our traveling example to Requirement 6 of our Leadership Wheel. It was not my intention to inspire others to track down their family trees. But inspiration occurred as people I met began their own searches as a new mission was formed to help others avoid losing their history.

As your team and company develop a greater good, be prepared to shift your mission. This transformation should be expected and embraced rather than avoided. The greater good for your company will shape over time. Striving for greatness means objectives, processes and policies will need to be perfected along the way. As the leader, team and company continue to care for this highest segment of the Wheel, improvement and adaptation should be an anticipated part of the process. As the greater good develops, there will be more defined activity for the quest of growing these company initiatives.

Requirement 6 Grows your Team

I was achieving elite success as a procurement from a cause people were identifying with. My new mission of providing individuals with their own opportunity to look into their family histories was also providing motivation to help in my research. While I wasn't finding answers, the activities of searching for the desired results were elite and far beyond what I'd envisioned accomplishing on my own.

Without speaking Polish or German, I was able to communicate enough of my story to result in people expending individual effort to help in my search. This is essentially the catalyst of achieving Requirement 6 on our Leadership Wheel. The lesson is simple. While you should celebrate an individual's efforts to catch a whale on their own, it takes a large team working together to do so.

The best way to expand your efforts outside of your team is to have a motivational cause associated with your mission. While the cause may be altruistic, it is more common for motivation to form around the growth of the company for greater opportunity, advancement and income of the employees. This could be accomplished through company stock, shared earnings and various incentives as recognition. The right mission will not only be sought by your team while you are not around, but it will have your Triple-A team expending energy prior to their start dates. Furthermore, employee's outside of your team and the sales organization will strive to make their own contributions.

The best example of support raised outside of your team will come from your service partners. While operational partnerships should be implemented regardless of any type of mission, the emotion behind their contributions is what makes adding a sales process to operations a huge success. Service partners have the ability to push for current client upgrades, referral programs and provide large contributions to your team. They may be the force to uncover current clients that can help build a national account or franchise relationship.

In order to get the proper endorsement and support from your customer service team, you should discuss your mission with the operational manager. Most often, your service partners are not required to sell. So, your network with these internal partners will help foster the reinforcement you need.

A solid partnership will allow you to get involved on a different level. You will be able to request speaking time during service meetings. This will allow you five to ten minutes to coach the service representatives on how to ask for referrals with happy customers, teach word tracks to solicit upgrades, launch programs and recognize the service reps succeeding in these sales activities. All of this exponentially grows your sales team outside of your direct reports. And frequently, the most recognized service members for these tasks get added to your Triple-A team.

Operations can be one of your largest contributors to new leads and additional revenue. Are you posting new word tracks on their computers for them to read at the conclusion of every call? Where else are you able to expand your sales team? Take time to think about these questions to strategically plan for the greater good. It cannot be achieved alone.

Rejection Becomes Enjoyable

Since Requirement 6 will have a greater purpose and meaning, elite leaders will find these goals colliding with a new level of dedication and activity to the tasks at hand. Swinging for the fences to grow the company becomes a norm because there is greater purpose to going through the failure. Rejection might be imminent, but it is the only way to push forward to the intended results of this segment.

Because there is a motivational cause behind the activity, the rejection becomes a source of pride and accomplishment. This is the stage where a kick in the teeth can actually be enjoyed. It wasn't abnormal for me to be finding fulfillment without answers, because I was searching for a heightened cause.

While my entire team of helpers were going through the same rejection, they remained even more positive than myself. They understood the opportunity and joy of providing my family the knowledge of our history and were individually taking on this activity for their own families as well. I'd once again found another theme as the motivation behind the greater good propelled an urgency for continued activity. Each person who helped me without success encouraged me with three words. "Don't give up."

There was encouragement in their voice and sincerity in their faces. They were coming along with me on my mission and continued to help in any way they could. Months after my travels, I found myself reaching out to numerous people I'd interacted with to update them on my story and continued search. I was met with thankful responses and continued encouragement.

Continued Team Expansion is Required

The Marquardt hardware store owner was another swing and a miss. Ayfer and I went to meet him to inquire if there was any relation. I ended up talking to the man's daughter on the phone as she spoke English and played translator for us. Renate later met us to be a part of the adventure as well. Once again, these people passionately wanted to help my cause and spent over an hour discussing my story. Despite not being related, the business owner started searching for Marquardt's in a regional phone book to no avail in an attempt to find new leads for my search.

The following day was our meeting with Martin and the enjoyment continued. We were invited into his home to visit, eat pie and were supplied with numerous online options to continue my search. While we didn't walk away with direct answers, I now have a better idea of how to investigate other avenues online when I am back in the United States.

While the two meetings did not produce immediate results, they felt more productive than what we were able to do on our own. We walked into small churches and random buildings in search of town archives. Not only were we striking out, but we got ourselves lost on more than one occasion.

Our time and effort in the surrounding towns of Calau was abundant, the results were not. While cold calling can often produce a positive outcome, it does not yield the highest return on investment. I was proud of my expanded efforts from the people that contributed to my search, but I, ultimately, did not have a big enough team to gain the result I was looking for.

When the desired results in your quest for the greater good goes unreached, the inevitable answer is to grow your efforts by expanding your team. Your network will provide other teams, top sales performers, operations, recruiters and the training department all working towards your mission of expanding opportunity within the sales organization. With a tactical pursuit, team expansion will occur as continued efforts are made in pursuit of the goal. What inspiration will you provide to rally around your mission?

There is no denying this level of elite leadership will provide passion for individuals inside and outside of your team. As you strive for this objective, you will need to grow awareness to build an army fighting for your vision. Elite leaders are able to influence the masses to get behind a cause and pursue it until it is achieved. Therefore, the leader's role for the top segment of the Wheel is achieved through proper preparation and motivation to create a relentless movement. The end result will positively impact the entire company.

It is equally important to remember your employees come first as you build all aspects of the Leadership Wheel. No one is interested in career advancement opportunities if they are not hitting their quota. They are trying to survive without getting fired or searching for an alternative company.

The process must start by your individual contributions to growth and learning for each member of your team. These are the people who will effectively mold and change the processes to achieve this top requirement of the Wheel. It cannot be accomplished by one leader as the passion for the cause must stem from the individuals on your team.

Prior to moving on to our final chapter, it is important to plan accordingly for the entire Leadership Wheel. While the top two levels of the Wheel are arduous tasks to achieve without accomplishing the first four requirements, leaders should envision their team at the top. What three things are you able to implement on your team today for the greater good of the company's future?

1. _____

   _____

2. _____

   _____

3. _____

   _____

These three items could come from any of our previous chapters and any requirement of the Wheel. As we head into our last chapter, you now have a better understanding of what is necessary for an elite leader to develop themselves and their team. Re-reading each portion of Markwardt's Wheel of Leadership will help you detail in on what is most needed by your team today.

17

King and Queen Markwardt

No one will ever inspire their team through personal accolades. You inspire your team by showing them how awesome they can be. They may not be able to envision what they will achieve, but leaders are able to help others believe in themselves in a whole new light. The single greatest factor in elite success is perseverance. Your guidance, support and encouragement in the right direction will help them stay the course.

Even though Ayfer and I left Calau with no more answers than I began with, this shared experience brought us closer together. Through my research, I stumbled on a village in East Germany named Marquardt. Furthering my interest is a castle known as Schloss Marquardt inside the town. While I have been unable to find the origin of the name, my curiosity is peaked. Ayfer is encouraging me to add this romanticized destination to my family search. Her support for what I'm trying to accomplish means the world to me, and it is helping me persevere to a new location after disappointment on our extensive search.

While I am having trouble tracing my family history back to the early 1900s, we are now headed to an area established in the fourteenth century. Not only is it getting more and more unlikely I will figure out where my family is from, it feels near impossible to trace my family back to this town and castle. But the possibility makes the trip an exciting adventure. My family and this castle are both from East Germany. And my surname is the name of the castle, town and on numerous signs as we travel to this little-known village outside of Berlin.

After spending significant time and energy not finding my family history, I am having fun envisioning my ancestors sipping tea in the courtyard of the castle on a warm summer day. We stop the car frequently so I can take a picture next to each Marquardt sign. We must be getting close as we listen to the GPS telling me to turn onto Marquardter Chaussee. A few minutes later, we park the car next to the castle.

It is an unusual day to navigate ourselves into the castle as people are headed to the estate for a black-tie affair. And, unfortunately, we aren't wearing the right clothes to blend into the crowd. But if we are going to view any part of this castle, we will be crashing what we learn is a wedding ceremony and reception to follow.

I'd traveled a long way with nothing to show for my family history other than what felt like less knowledge than I'd originally started with. Hence, there isn't a thought of not venturing into the venue. As we walk onto the castle grounds, we see the wedding ceremony is about to start on the lawn facing the lake. The timing of our entry benefits us as the castle is only occupied by the catering company, workers and the wedding coordinator.

I walk through the front door and flash my business card to the first person I see. "Hi. My name is Jon Markwardt, and my last name used to be spelled with a q when my family was in Germany. I'm not sure if there is any relation to this castle, but I want to look around." At this point of my search, I believe there is no reason I couldn't be a descendant from the castle.

The man half chuckles. "Just a minute. You'll need to speak with the wedding coordinator."

I am fortunate he speaks English as he brings over a lady who appears to be quite busy. But with a hesitant blessing and smile, I am allowed to snap a few photos around the castle as long as I do not disturb any of their guests as the reception inside hasn't started.

We leave the castle feeling triumphant and explore the surrounding park, the lake and a church. We walk into a convenience store, and I am able to purchase Marquardt postcards and two small books on the history of the town of Marquardt. It is a small consolation prize from my search that will provide entertaining gifts for my family when I return home. But the books are in German, so it doesn't do me a whole lot of good at the moment. I'd eventually need to track down this history as my curiosity is getting the best of me. I want to say my ancestors owned a castle!

I fall in love with this being my family story. And Ayfer decides to believe this tall tale as she starts calling me her king. In the moment, I embrace the most positive ending to my voyage. We laugh all the way to Berlin about my castle, crashing the wedding and my change in fortune. A king of a castle has a much better ring to it than the funeral home I found in Calau.

I wish I could end the book as King Markwardt, but I'd prefer to act with intellectual honesty. My later research proved my royalty otherwise. In 1704, Marquard Ludwig von Printzen became the lord, landowner and namesake of the town and castle. Marquard was his first name, so I would not be able to claim the castle as part of my history. Furthering my frustration was the guy's name didn't even have a "t" on the end of it. I couldn't figure out why the town and castle did. I am so far off from finding my family history; I feel like giving up.

"Be the King of an awesome attitude!"

Perseverance

Part of having the ability to persevere is knowing when to take a break. Sales, leadership and life offers different paths that all lead to success. And when you continually run into a brick wall with one, it's advantageous to change directions. Your attitude and sanity will thank you.

This may mean cutting your losses on an employee working hard but not translating their activity into results. You must create a culture demanding dependability. If there is an individual who cannot be counted on to produce, they are hurting the rest of the team if they are allowed to stay around. Thus, your perseverance for the betterment of the team must now fixate on replacing the underperforming individual.

Leaders are successful for what they do and don't do. While a manager might continue to force effort into someone due to their own stubbornness or ego, a leader will do what is best for the team. This includes admitting when a poor hire is made or the wrong activity was given as the direction for the team to follow.

The humbleness and humanness of being a leader includes making mistakes. Share these mistakes with your team and navigate elsewhere. And in my own story, it was time to change routes for the time being. After an exhausting search in Calau and the surrounding towns with Ayfer, I would be flying out of Berlin in four days. And on our drive from the castle into Berlin, I relinquished any further research on my family during our remaining time together.

I was shifting my focus, and I needed to do so. I was disappointed with how the research panned out as I would not return home with answers. But right in front of me stood someone I had an amazing connection with, and I owed it to myself to invest my remaining time and energy into us prior to heading back home.

A New Greater Good

The quest for the greater good, as discussed, requires an openness to change. Essentially, this falls right in line with the ability for any individual to persevere by shifting focus to achieve a similar or greater result. Over my remaining days in Germany, I altered my agenda.

Despite one's experience, knowledge or skill set; it is hard to shift focus. We all want to achieve the desired outcome we search for. But my new greater good was no longer about family histories. It was about Ayfer, and it was about us. My previous quest had a special meaning to myself and family. But this new journey had even more significance to myself and the impact it would have on my life and those around me.

At the time, it didn't seem possible for our relationship to be more than travel companionship during a paramount part of my voyage. But as our time progressed to the end in Berlin, it was hard to deny the connection we had and the unique experience we shared together. While I never found the answers to the questions on my family, I'd found something more important as I believed our lives would be better together than apart.

A leader must be able to adapt and change for elite success and a greater good to occur for their team. Quite often, the most optimal result is not the conclusion we envision. For myself, good fortune had been created by allowing another opportunity to unfold. The lesson on shifting focus is not to give up on your original mission. Throwing in the towel is much different than changing your pursuit of excellence when a greater opportunity arises.

Drastic Change

My arms wrap around Ayfer for our final embrace. My taxi is outside the hotel, and I need to head to the airport. As the tears roll down my face and hers, I can't even utter the words to say goodbye. I put on my sunglasses to cover my eyes and quietly walk out to the street and get into the taxi. As I sit in the taxi contemplating my decision to leave, I decide to start planning a move to Istanbul.

While changing focus may be one of the hardest tasks of leadership, I can share through my own experience that it can be the most rewarding. My previous quest was identifiable to everyone else as providing a greater good. New opportunities were formed as countless individuals began to search for their family history. But my new journey could provide a similar and more drastic opportunity, personally, by joining our lives together.

I flew back to Minnesota with a small stay in Chicago before arriving to see family and friends in a familiar setting. My travels felt like they were incomplete with my impending desire to be in Istanbul with Ayfer. However, months before I'd even planned my trip, I'd made a promise to one of my closest friends, Sascha Bunster, I intended to keep. We had become friends in San Diego, and he was the biggest San Diego Chargers fan I knew. When his team announced their move out of the city, I made a promise and commitment to adopt him as a Minnesota Vikings fan.

A dependable leader is as important as a dependable friend. I'd bought tickets to the first game of the year, and I promised Sascha I'd take him to the game with me. Suitably, it wasn't a hard decision for me to continue with my planned events. Ayfer encouraging me to do so provided me with greater confirmation for my desire to continue our relationship.

Multiple Levels to the Greater Good

While we discussed variant aspects of the greater good, we simplify it here as there is a wide range to this spectrum. It does not need to change the world, your company or life. Sometimes it is as simple as showing up for a friend in Minnesota when you wanted to continue your travels to Istanbul.

The greater good is defined as creating additional opportunities for those around you, regardless of what that opportunity might be. The task of restructuring the sales organization to create expanded roles and positions is quite arduous, but an elite leader will persevere to this upper echelon of pushing company growth. Elite leaders will also continuously form smaller opportunities for their team.

At the lowest level of building the greater good into your team, a leader is able to create opportunities on a smaller scale. This may include building a booth for your representatives to gain clients at a trade show. It could be expensing a college course for an employee to continue their education. The list goes on as leaders creatively expand opportunities for the individuals on their team.

These opportunities do not need to come as direct programs from the company. An elite leader will create them and may use their own money to provide their employees with extended learning and growth. As a leader, there is no greater investment than investing in your employees.

Minnesota was the right decision as I fulfilled my promise to a friend. Sascha and I watched the Vikings win their

As a leader, there is no greater investment than investing in your employees.

first game of the year. We had a blast! While the San Diego Chargers leaving his hometown was devastating to him, we were both excited to be cheering on the Vikings together. This opportunity brought us closer as we now share enthusiasm for the same team.

Wheels Never End

While I was in Minnesota, I was able to spend time with my parents and grandparents sharing the details of my travels and discoveries along the way. We continued the family search at my grandpa's home in St. Paul. And I used the online searches I'd learned from Martin in Calau, Germany to locate boat records.

This pin-pointed my great-grandfather's immigration to May of 1912. Not only did the records document he was of German heritage with a mother of Berta Markwart, but it further detailed his current citizenship as Russian. This follows the German family document citing Rudolph and his father traveled from Russia to the United States.

I was even able to find a boat document with Adolph returning months later on a different boat. Thus, it gave him time to return to his family at the end of 1912, which would coincide with his untimely death in 1913. This all gave way to the most believable evidence I was able to produce on a timeline for my family entering the United States and where they came from. My grandfather enjoyed the opportunity to learn more about the events his father scarcely discussed.

"Everyone enjoys being on top. But celebrating the journey is the true victory."

While the results weren't exactly what I was searching for, one thing was clear. My search and quest for finding my family history is not over. A quest for the greater good is most often not achieved. Professionally, even once it is accomplished, it is constant work to maintain and continue to build all aspects of the Leadership Wheel.

Two months after leaving Berlin, I started a personal chapter for the greater good. Ayfer and I met in Amsterdam to celebrate Halloween where we dressed up as the King and Queen. Afterwards, we traveled together to my new home in Istanbul.

Istanbul is where our own journey has continued. And the new opportunities we've found in each other have been endless. Four months after moving to Turkey, I proposed to Ayfer Metin, and she accepted the engagement. We were married just months later in St. Anthony's church in Istanbul. Our story will continue with our impending travel to the United States as a married couple.

As I look out at the sun setting over the Bosphorus water next to the famous Blue Mosque, I can attest to my greatest accomplishment in leadership being the ability to enjoy the journey above the end result. This is the key ingredient to fulfillment in your position as a wheel and leadership quest have no end. Safe and happy travels to each of you on your voyage!

Acknowledgments

Thank you to my aunt, Lissa Markwardt, for the continued memory of my uncle, Gary Markwardt. Lissa has been a proponent of living your life now and following your dreams as her husband's life was taken from us far too early. As a tribute and a way to keep his memory alive, I have embraced my aunt's challenge and am living my life now.

To Steve Junor, thank you for listening to my story, providing inspiration and encouraging me to take this journey. Your text messages throughout my travels provided me with energy each day. And when things didn't go well, you helped me find the humor in my failures. Failing is a part of life, so we can choose to find the joy in it or expand the disappointment. Thank you for spreading the joy with each person you meet.

To Ron and Devonne Markwardt, thank you for supporting me in all I do. I couldn't have asked for better cheerleaders as parents. Your belief in me helped give me the confidence to take a different path with my career. I am thankful to enjoy what I do each day and fulfill my dream of inspiring others.

To my grandfather, Ken Markwardt, thank you for your encouragement and ability to share insight from a business perspective. Your stories and our business conversations have provided me with wise advice over the years. Thank you for continuing to push my urgency for success to a peak level.

To my mentor, Tom Riley, thank you for still being the first person I call as my trusted advisor. I altered the outline of this book in Cyprus with your encouragement, and it quickly became the right decision to write this book through the Leadership Wheel. As the book's first reader, you became part of the story as you helped shape the final copy being read today.

To Nicki Pack, thank you for your advice on my travels through Istanbul. Not only did my entire book change by meeting Ayfer, but you changed my life in a way that I will never be able to repay you. Thank you for your generosity and kindness to both of us.

To Ayfer Markwardt, thank you for helping me re-write my story and effectively our own stories at the same time. There will never be enough chapters in our book of life, so I'm going to enjoy every chapter we're blessed to share. I love you.

To my Poland relatives, Krzysztof and Ewelina Kordas, I will never forget you welcoming me into your home as family and our conversations through my computer to translate the meaning of our words. Your help and effort to track down my family history was beyond what I could have ever expected.

To Eugenia Perechuda, thank you for keeping family records to provide additional knowledge and leads on our family tree. Your letters to the United States were a testimony to the importance of family, and were well received throughout the years. Without your correspondence, I would have never known where to begin this journey.

To Bob Carr, thank you for taking the time to share your insight on leadership and your continued drive for success. You are an inspiration for anyone who reads this book and a true example of what leadership means.

To Taavi Rõivas, thank you for inviting me into the Estonian Parliament Building. Your dedication to growth and learning for your country is admirable and should be imitated around the world. Your humbleness allowed you to surround yourself with the best possible people, which provides you great strength as a leader.

To Nona Mamulashvili, thank you for your time and insight in Tbilisi on the challenges you face and how you overcome them. While each of us may feel unfairness, there are people in this world who face true prejudice and it can often derail the most qualified leaders. Your dedication to the enjoyment of the challenge and treating these situations as a game provides motivation and hope for all to no longer be discouraged.

To Penelope Constantinou, thank you for your friendship and joining me again on this journey of my second book. Your sketches helped tell my story in the way a talented artist only could. I'm thankful for your support and continue to wish you great success.

To Kelly Henderson, thank you for designing the Leadership Wheel to make my vision come to life. Your ability to design the Wheel better than I envisioned showcased your strength as a graphic designer.

To Arda Aytan, thank you for your patience to capture the perfect photograph for the back cover of this book. You helped add a fun and important message to each reader.

To my publishing company and the entire team who worked tirelessly to create a book to help grow leaders, thank you. Leaders are relied on to positively impact lives. May this book be a compounding equation for those who read it.

To everyone who contributed to my travels and stories along the way: Crina Barbu, Kerim Barutçu, Paschal Bay, Kate and Michael Holmes, Nino Imnadze, Liisa Jonninen, Ceren Kutukcu, Ismail Kirmaci, Anna Łagowska, Diana Lemke, Niko Loz Lekveishvili, Gökhan Mandir, Evie and Michalis Michael, Mia Pirttilä, Nicola Satori, Christopher Simonet, Martin Strödicke, Ludmila and Dariusz Szulski, Ave Tampere, Baris Taptik, Renate Uckrow, and everyone who joined me playing Finnish baseball.

Thank you to everyone who has helped influence and form my own leadership career: Rich Adams, Julian Ballesteros, Tyler Bartholomew, Jorden Bastien, Mark Bottini, Erin Brown, Ivan Camacho, Todd Cassell, Lawrence Chavez, Phil Coria, Crystal Cozad, Larry Farin, Cardedrick Foreman, Katrina Galvan, Cliff Gibson, Kim Gibson, Tom Hall, Randy Holyfield, Casey Ingram, Miguel A. de Jesus, Angel Jones, Ryan Joswick, Jay Kennel, Gabrielle Knott, Mike Leland, Steve Lewis, Zack Lockhart, Lois Makely, Jessica Marcinko, Erin Martin, Cindy Matalucci, Steve McKensie, Matt Miller, Scott Moore, Erek Newton, David O'Day, Chad Preuss, Marcus Ray, Amy Roberts, Lisa Robinson, Nathan Rutledge, Bill Schuffenhauer, Tiffany Sirikulvadhana, Pam Slater, Jon Slywiak, Rahul Thathoo, Ryan Thorne, Jerry Vitovsky, Justin Volrath, Jason Wagg, Steve Weidman, Justin Wheeler, Mike Whelan, Lisa Williams, Chris Witte.

To my Friends and family who continually support me along my journey no matter what turn I take: Shevy, Erika, Krimzen, Brooklyn, Regan and Crew Akason, Melinda Anderson, Brendan and Shauna Bligh, Mike and Kim Boecher, Larry and Janice

Bradfield, Sascha and Jessica Bunster, Tom and Mary Campbell, Dan and Mariko Dahl, Scott and Jen Engel, Matt Halvorson, Derek and Tina Hill, Nick and Amy Jacobson, Steve and Leslie Junor, Brad and Jean Krasean, Bernice Markwardt, Bryan Markwardt, Jeff Markwardt, Kenny and Jenn Markwardt, Tom and Nancy Markwardt, Jessica Montgomery, Mihowe Oprzadek, Lyndsey Parker, Ryan and Emily Richard, Jake and Molly Rodenbiker, Scott Rosecrans, Zain Tejani, Nick and Amanda Thompson and Drew Visconti.

I conclude my acknowledgments with an apology for those whose names were not placed in writing. I believe we get the opportunity to learn and grow from every person we interact with, so thank you to those who have contributed to my growth both personally and professionally. You know who you are. Thank you!

About the Author

Jon Markwardt lived in Istanbul while working on the publication of this book. To write this book on leadership, he traveled through twelve different countries over six months, interviewed three recognized leaders and spent endless hours researching and writing. His dedication to this book served his mission to educate and grow more leaders in the sales community.

Markwardt currently travels for speaking events as a retention expert for businesses along with attending functions to promote his books and educate those in the sales profession. His larger mission is to inspire everyone he meets to learn and grow. He believes there is no greater investment than investing in yourself. But in an age of instant gratification, greater numbers are relying on technology over their own commitment to growth. His goal is to change this trend as he writes and speaks in a non-traditional manner to provide entertainment surrounding education.

His title for his books claim the *Grass Is Browner*. This mantra on life encourages everyone to enjoy their current moment as all they have. By watering your lawn, you can have the greenest grass on the block. While some situations inevitably require some to change their yard, this philosophy is a push to encourage all to make the most of their position. The key to success and happiness thus ends up being a choice, and it is a decision he encourages us to make each and every day for your career and personal life.

Markwardt's work history includes thirteen years of selling and leadership positions for two Fortune 1000 companies along with building and scaling a sales, service and business development division for a start-up company in Silicon Valley. His true passion is coaching and inspiring people to new heights in their current roles. Consequently, he is recognized as one of the nation's top retention experts and continues to be interviewed on the topic of millennials in the workforce.

Markwardt was born in Fargo, North Dakota. He attended Augustana University and graduated from the University of San Diego. Jon and Ayfer were married less than a year after they met in Istanbul. Together, they traveled as a married couple post their wedding to make their home in the United States.

The outline for Markwardt's next book has been written as a guide to elite networking. Travel plans are being made, and Ayfer will join the next voyage. To stay up-to-date on speaking events, articles, tips, advice and the destination for his next book, please go to GrassIsBrowner.com to sign up for his free newsletter. You can contact Jon through the website to arrange a speaking event or provide your own testimonial.

Markwardt's Wheel of Leadership

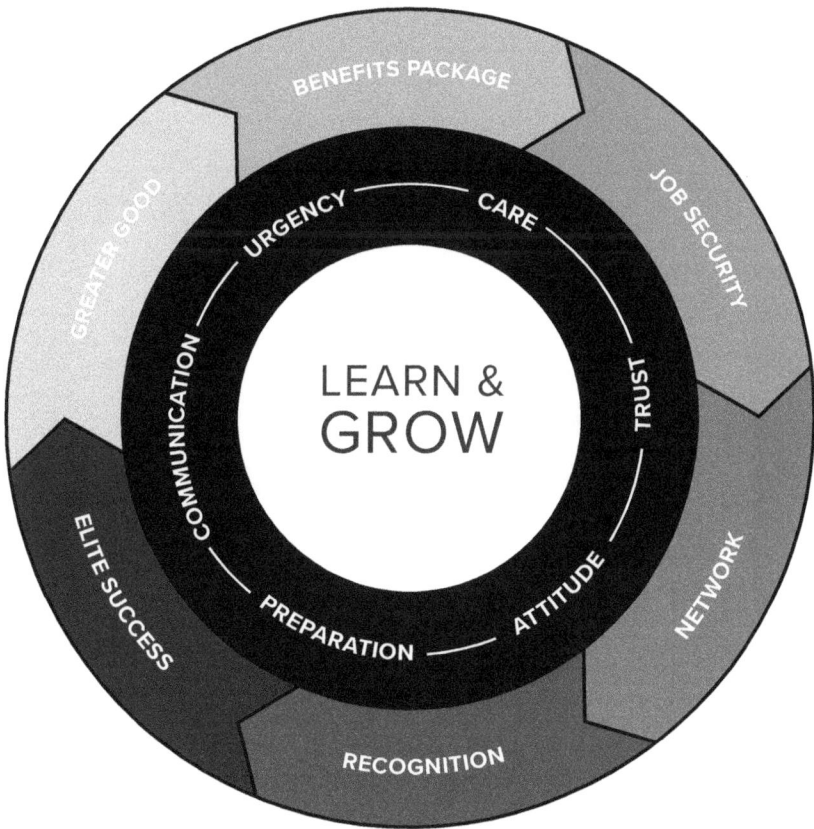

www.ingramcontent.com/pod-product-compliance
Lightning Source LLC
Chambersburg PA
CBHW022055210326
41519CB00054B/411